# Dreams, Past Lives, Holy Spirits, Your Soul!

ISBN: 1-58820-273-9

This book is printed on acid free paper.

1st Books - rev. 10/3/02

# CONTENTS

# ACKNOWLEDGEMENTS

I do thank my loving spiritual partner Will Griffith. Without his love, and support I would not of had to do what I am now doing for myself, and others. I also want to thank various teachers (see my bibliography) for all their informative messages, and truths they have shared. I want to thank my daughter, Leah, for helping me get free. My son, Owen, for his understanding and letting me help him with his self-realization. I would like to thank Judy Nelsen for helping me start a spiritual recovery, and discovery program here in the Columbia River Gorge. I send my thanks out to Puma for helping me formulate my new soul name. I also send thanks out to Doreen Virtue PhD, for telling me at one of her workshops that I was great, great priestess. Thanks for all the Hypnotherapy programs available for Medical, and Spiritual healing and personnel transformation. I also want to thank my Mom and Dad for having faith in me through all the rough times.

# FORWARD

We are living in an extraordinary time. The 21$^{st}$ century has brought with it a remarkable resurgence of interest in Spirituality and the duality of the self. A new generation of seekers is emerging with many questions that need to be answered. The first and most critical one is, "Where do I begin?" Now thanks to the work of Lynn-Mystic Healer, we have the answer. <u>DREAMS, PAST LIVES, HOLY SPIRITS, YOUR SOUL</u> is an excellent "jump-off" place for those wishing to navigate the water of the spirit. Use this book to start your journey, and *bon voyage!*

R.A. Neves, PhD.

President ABH= American Board of Hypnotherapy

# INTRODUCTION

Why am I writing this book? I have found through my work, that people must learn how to get in touch with God within. My work with Spiritual Hypnotherapy has proven over and over that when people are having a problem, their Holy Spirits (divine guides) can guide them to health, prosperity, love, joy, and peace. We all have Holy Spirits that are connected to our breath. Our Breath is connected to our soul. Everyone's soul is connected to God.

SOUL GUIDES By Lynn Mystic-Healer

Find your soul guides to get into your flow
Let the fearful loathing ego go-
We all have cosmic Holy Spirits waiting
Rise above your illness through meditating

THERE IS ONLY ONE GOD ONE GOD
RELIGIONS UNITE STOP THE FIGHTS
Our Breath is our soul-we are all connected here
  you know-
To the same love and light that has all insight
Brothers and sisters unite-yes, unite
Religions teach inner self-love from the light
Connect to god your heart will delight
Our hearts already know what is right

There is enough money to share
Hear your truth within your call not despair
Come forth and spread more love not fear

THERE IS ONLY ONE GOD –ONE GOD-

Religions unite the time is right
Religions unite stop the fights

I want to dedicate this book to my children and all other people of the world that have endured loss, suffering, or trauma, of mind or body. This book is for all people who are hurting emotionally or physically. I also want to help all the people in jail and in the psychiatric wards. It is a fact that 95% of all the people in jails, chronic care units of the hospitals, and mental institutes are people suffering from psychosomatic-disorders. The jails and mental institutes are filled with drug/and or alcohol disorders. When there is a problem you can trace it back to lack of self-love, and lack of love for others. Disconnected people are not coping well.

This is a new millennium. The earth has come to a time of critical choice. It is time to reconnect to GOD. God is so much bigger than the internet. It is time to remember how to connect to the energy of God. All religions must unite to stop all the fighting and human suffering. There are enough monies in the defense departments, drugs, alcohol, gambling and sports activities, and religious buildings throughout the world to save the world. These monies could be reallocated to the humanitarian services.

People of this planet must learn how to come from their God given divine direction first. We have strayed so far from our spirit connection to God. The Old Testament goes back to Adam and Eve. God asked Adam and Eve not to eat the fruit of the forbidden tree. God has tried to explain the cause and effect of this choice. When Eve chose to eat of this fruit of knowledge she let go of her direct link to God. When Adam chose to eat the fruit of knowledge he also broke his direct link to God. This is when mankind started to use his brain before consulting God. Religions started growing all over the world trying to get in touch with God again. The more religions put time into their buildings, and getting money, and following scriptural books, and doing their own interpretations of their copy of various bibles, the further they got from their heart's truth. God is not attached to our brain. God is not attached to a book. God is attached to our soul. Our soul is attached to our breath. When someone dies, that person's soul (spirit) goes off into the universe with his or her breath.

The Bible was written 80 years after Jesus was born. Jesus was only alive for 33 years. His teachings are blessed and immortal. Jesus was a Son of God. Jesus tried to tell people not to idolize him. He wanted to help people get in touch with God. Jesus was trying to teach people how to reconnect with God. All people are connected to God by their soul. We are all children of God. We have free choice. We have free will. We have forgotten how to connect to God in our daily lives. Our minds, our finite brains, are attached to free will, and EGO. Our minds get attached to fear. Our minds remember all negative emotions, and painful situations. Our minds hold onto anger, violence, lust, greed, shame, terror, rage, revenge, and various other negative situations. Our thoughts create our realities. The more we keep our thoughts on negative emotions, negative situations, and negative behaviors the worse we feel. When we do not feel well we tend to self-medicate, and make poor choices. This is how all kinds of bad habits get started. Fearful thoughts need to be let go to God, so God help you. Learn how to meditate when feeling off balance, not self-medicate. God is not in a book. God is inside of you.

All the major religions of the world must learn to teach Love. Our spirit connects us all to God, by our breath. We all have a beautiful, fun reason to be alive now. Our soul's connection to God is eternal. All the master spiritual teachers came here to teach people how to connect with the omniscient powers of God inside each of us. God is also omnipresent. GOD IS LOVE, AND LIGHT ENERGY. This Love and light energy is cosmic. In Physics it is about relativity of matter, energy. Our mind is not our soul. Our minds are like an open computer at birth. Our minds take in all they see, hear, smell, touch, and taste. This information is stored as we grow up from a baby. Our society has gotten so far away from knowing how to connect with our souls that our planet is in trouble.

"It is to peace that God has called you...Let each of you lead the life that the Lord has assigned, to which God called you."- 1Corinthians 7:15, 17

This book is being written to let you know there is a way to talk to God yourself. You can learn how to hear, see, and feel God. I am also writing to let people know to have faith in themselves, have faith in their own visions, and understand their own dreams. When you Love yourself, you give off a vibration of love, this vibration in turn will get the "right" love for you. Opposites only attract for a short time. Like attracts like, birds of a feather will flock together, or the physics of cause and effect.

God can help you learn to love yourself. When you love what you do, you find others like you. Only God truly knows what is best for you. God is omniscient, and omnipresent for you. Hypnosis with a spiritual counselor can help you access this energy plane.

# MY PAST, MY HEALING

A few years ago, I did not understand the Bible. Parts of the Bible I knew were not for me. Some parts of the Bible are wrong for me. Some parts of the Bible are inappropriate for me. I did not believe in God. I did not understand any of the major religions' beliefs about a higher power. I was not going to go to this level of supernatural beliefs. I did not want to believe in God. I found that most churches were fighting, or competing amongst themselves. The feelings I picked up around churches were far from loving. I found most organized religions to be hypocritical, and self-serving. I found churches asking for donations and free labor, and helping very few. I found churches where the needy were treated as if they were not good enough to attend. I found churches judging each other quite critically throughout the entire congregation. I found preachers teaching all kinds of personal interpretations of God that were not loving to their congregations. I also found more negative, dooming, and fearful sermons. As if the world did not have enough problems the rest of the week.

My life was so full of suffering. I truly felt there could not be so much human suffering if there was a God. Why go to church to feel more pain and worse about your life? Why go to church if someone there wants to make you feel more shame, or more guilt? I was suffering enough; I needed help, not more negative feelings.

I had gone through many phases of addictions, and chronic body complaints. I spent time as a smoker, a drug addict, an alcoholic, a "wino," anorexic, bulimic.

I was paranoid and I had suffered deep grief (when I lost my closest brother at age 17). My older brothers went to Viet Nam. I felt fear and distaste inside my bones over the meaningless use of that war to settle problems and the tragedies affiliated with lack of caring communication. I kept pondering how the power and egos running the war were from just a handful of mean, men-children. I did not understand the lack of tolerance, and inability to care, and share, and help one another. I also experienced other types of depressions and anxieties, and have experienced many other human traumas, and dilemmas. I have empathy for all emotional and physical human ailments.

I was mentally and physically abused for years as a fearful co-dependant wife. My ex-husband was a bi-sexual, drug addict, con. His choices and actions, and behaviors were bizarre to me. His power, money and threats towards my children and me kept me imprisoned. I definitely had periods of mania, and deep depression, bi-polar periods. I experienced other schizophrenia type phases during my abuse, and subsequent drug use. What was happening to me was insane, the drugs just made it numb. I did not know how to get out of the cycle. I did not know how to get my power back. I did not know where to turn to get help. A voice deep inside kept saying, "Get free to be. Get free to become yourself. Free yourself from all the negative energy relationships."

My daily relationship to these thoughts, feelings and people I was with was killing me. My only escape was drugs, and drinking. Slowly, but inevitably the drugs, and alcohol made matters worse. I then realized that losing myself to stop all the bad feelings was also creating problems and distance with my kids. Then guilt and shame came, so more horrible feelings had to be stopped, "numbed." I begged for changes, and pleaded and urged to get counseling. The more I tried to make everyone else happy the worse I became. I was becoming an enabler out of fear, and I hated my life.

My RN psychiatric background kept me going, saying there is another way out. There is another way to release bad feelings. My heart kept saying, "You must get away from your bad relationships. You are lost, and need to go find your self. Go and find a healthy lifestyle." I knew it was not through sitting around talking endlessly about all my problems. I knew the old way of psychological, analytical babble-- going on, and on about more and more complaints and problems was not the way to heal.

What you put thought and energy on grows. So conventional psychotherapy was out. I knew it was not through more or different drugs. I had enough drugs for a lifetime, or two or three. Which way out? Divorce was scary, and painful, and I nearly got killed two times. Within six weeks of the divorce, I had gone cold turkey from all drugs, and alcohol. With the use of vitamins, good nutrition, lots of liquid, and exercise, I had no withdrawals, but I was still caught in old thoughts, and tempting habits. What to do with my life? Where will I fit?

I was looking hard for a way out of my old thoughts, painful memories, and life situations, when God sent me information about how to transform my life with Hypnotherapy. My inner guide said, "You must check this out. What do you have to lose?" Just go and see what it is about.

I signed up immediately for this Hypnotherapy program. As soon as I signed up, I felt better. I was so looking forward to this program. There was now a passion that was welling up inside of me that had not been with me for years. Just the anticipation from signing up was terrific. I was astonished with the incredible feelings of relief, and transformation that was happening to me. Everyone in the program was a bit like me. Most were looking for a better way to heal themselves, and learn more about their soul-mind-body connection. It was fun to follow my heart desire, and find people like myself in the program. I was learning so much about the energy systems of people. One of the students, and artists had been working with chakras for years. I was astounded to learn how our subconscious is attached to our spirituality.

I was not going to look at Past Life regressions. I did not believe in them. At this time, I still did not believe in God. At first, all I wanted to do was Post-traumatic stress relief work for myself, using Hypnosis. It worked wonders. The more we studied all the different levels, and uses of Hypnotherapy the more excited I became about the possibilities for true healing, and lasting changes. I immersed my self in studying and teaching Medical Hypnotherapy. What a wonderful healing modality.

I was working away with MEDICAL HYPNOTHERAPY Script work. These scripts were from PhDs, and various MDs. Some of these scripts were from the American Society of Clinical Hypnosis. I wanted to help people with addictions and chronic emotional problems. I wanted to help these people learn how to heal their lives. I was learning to heal mine. I found hypnotherapy to be life altering. I found it to be the way to make life choice changes. I found it to work wonders for many physical and emotional problems, with NO harmful side effects. It helped me so very much. I am so excited to share this life altering, fun, relaxing, enlightening process. Hypnotherapy is similar to a deep level of Meditation. It is like a brain massage; it feels so good to be in a trance state.

I was only going to pursue MEDICAL HYPNOTHERAPY, But after a NEAR DEATH EXPERIENCE, WHAM. God's Holy Spirits started coming to all my clients while they were in session. I was only doing medical hypnotherapy script release work. I was not going to do Spiritual Hypnotherapy. Not Me, Oh, no! My clients started to see, and talk to dead people, guardian angels, Jesus Christ, and other Saints, and ascended masters. These Holy spirits came to my clients, not to me. They knew exactly what to say to help them with all their secrets, and intimate questions. These Holy Spirits told my clients about all their PAST LIVES with them, and on and on. God's Holy Spirits knew exactly, perfectly, how and what each person needed to heal. These Holy Spirits knew what each client needed to do with their life to be happy. They knew everything about the client! They had been with the client many lives. The words omniscient and omnipresent became real. The Biblical stories about Jesus and God became alive. Buddhism also became real as did parts of the Torah. All kinds of information about higher power started to come into my life. The similarities of this God force that all the master religious, or spiritual teachers talk about is amazing. This cosmic higher power energy we can connect with is real, and it is full of love energy, and light energy.

Hypnotherapies, either Medical or Spiritual, are ways to change and heal your life by connecting with this divine energy. I knew for years that all the people in the mental institutes, jails, and chronic care facilities just needed a way to love themselves, to feel good about themselves and their lives. Happy people do not hurt themselves or others. True LOVE is what everyone needs. Hypnotherapy can open the doors to the subconscious, to your higher power, wisdom, joy, passion, truths and connectedness to real energy bonds with people of like-mindedness for your need to love and to belong. You can find out where you will be happy, and fit in on this earth plane. Learn how to love yourself and follow love, for miracles are happening daily for you to feel a part of.

You can learn how to become unlimited with help from your own omniscient God connection. Your true balance and flow are part of your spiritual (chakra) energy system. You can learn how to become more at ease with yourself, and others when you balance yourself with your soul's information, and guidance. This type of healthy balance naturally keeps you out of DIS-EASE. When you know how to stay comfortable (AT EASE) with your self, and others, you do not stress; you flow, and your life is healthier. God does not want us to be unhappy!

# PART ONE

# YOUR SOUL, YOUR BREATH is your connection to God

We are all connected to God via our breath. Our breath is part of our soul. All humans, and animals are connected to God via the holy breath. Our breath is holy. "In his hands is the life of every living thing and the breath of every human being."-Job 12:10. Women use their breath during labor and delivery for natural childbirth. I have used the breath to pull people out of shock in the emergency room in the Queen Charlotte Islands. The breath is also used during Hypnotherapy and Meditation.

People get hooked on cigarettes because of the breath. The intention behind taking a smoke break is to get space, clear a thought. The intention can be so deliberate that the brain goes quiet for a minute, and you listen for information. The truth is that the deliberate intention behind the smoke break was to ask for guidance. Therefore people equate smoking with this time-out for thoughts, and guidance. The real truth is you do not need to smoke to get this quiet time break. YOU most certainly do not need to smoke to get information from the universe. Deep, even, deliberate breathing is part of the opening of the chi energy, and soul connection. This breathing is part of the phone line, the "hook-up" to God.

Smoke breaks are a polluted way of a quick meditation. Tobacco Industries are making money on what is given to you to use freely, naturally. The yogis have known the best way to take a break in time is to deep breathe and relax into clear knowing. Do not waste your money on polluting your lungs with cigarettes. It is a rip off! Smoking also damages your lung tissues. The toxins used in the papers and processing of the tobacco are hard on your other vital organs and vascular system. It has been said smoking creates a dharma energy screen that blocks off good energy forces.

## HOW TO BREATHE:

The breath is Holy. All you need to do is learn to ask the universe to help you, then go into deep breathing and listen for your guidance. Take time to feel the calming effects of deep breathing. Breathe in through the nose as deeply as you can, as slowly as you can. Hold this breath for 3-4 counts then let it go slowly through pursed lips. The yogis have used the breath for centuries. Do this over, and over. It is physiologically impossible to deep breathe and be anxious at the same time.

Your life will change, if you learn to breathe through difficulties. Learn how to ask for help, breathe slowly, and deeply as mentioned, and listen to your divine guidance. Your lungs will be happier, and you will start to feel alive again. Good breathing breaks are a type of meditation. Meditation is the most important way to listen to God. All the major religions, including Christianity (Shalom) use meditation as a way of listening to God. The Bible also mentions meditation. The breath is the most neglected human element. The breath is more important than water or food. The breath is Holy and part of our soul.

# JAILS, MENTAL INSTITUTES, AND CHRONIC CARE PATIENTS

All these people are lost and disconnected from their spiritual truths. They do not know or believe that they can receive help from the universe. They are all looking outside of themselves for passion, love and happiness.

All the Highs from any drug are already inside your cells. God made you perfect just the way you are. You do not need drugs to make you happy. You do not need drugs to make you a better person. Drugs and alcohol are ruining our planet. Look inside the jails. How many cases are drug and alcohol related? 95 %. Wow! How many jails are being built today across the United States of America? Jails are growing faster than schools. How about all the people going to counseling, AA, Alanon groups, overeating groups, or other type of addiction recovery groups? How about our societies mental hospitals? How many of you know that drugs and/or alcohol put most of these people over the edge? People with eating disorders and long term chronic care patients are all unhappy, disconnected individuals. These unhappy people are looking outside for something to make them ok, feel good, or fit in.

Hypnotherapy can help you access your subconscious and your soul for transformational changes. You can transform your life, by using God's energy in you. You have Holy Spirits, angels, and master teachers waiting to help. You have dreams to help you. You can dowse for all kinds of answers from the universe. You can discover your past lives, and be taken into the light of God for your present life lessons.

Enlightenment comes from studying your eternal soul's information. You can astral travel. You can learn how to access the akashic records for unlimited soul wisdom. God can take you on the best, most exciting life journeys--far, far beyond any man made drugs, or alcohol.

## JAILS:

The majority of case histories concerning someone in jail show reasons for what they did. There are only about 5 % of people in jails that came here as Satan's children. These few came here to be hurtful. They have a history as young children to deliberately hurt innocent animals, and other children. They do not show remorse, they will not repent. They are cold, self–serving and they have no heart. Satan's children get their power from manipulation and hurting others. These people feed on the weakness of others. They only pretend to care for others; these people are "Cons."

These few tend to spoil it for the vast majority. The dark force must become enlightened, like a dark room that needs more light. Once someone flicks on the light, the darkness goes away. While the majority of humanity is lost or disconnected, all people are vulnerable. We look for a quick fix, and the dark temptations are everywhere.

Do this or that, and you will feel better. There is dark energy; there are dark people (Darth Vaders). People must become more aware of their feelings, so they do not get taken, abused, and mistreated. If you feel –'VIBES' that are strange -BE AWARE OF

THESE FEELINGS. Feel your feelings, understand your energy vibrations around you at all times, angels are near and giving you helpful signs everywhere. Wake up to all your sensations. Your feelings are important! Do not give your power away. When you take drugs/alcohol you are vulnerable to the dark forces. You cannot feel your true feelings.

Learn how to party naturally, the way God made you, perfect just as you are. Be aware of all your feelings, at social gatherings, your feelings are with you for a reason. You must learn to honor them, ask God to help you understand them better, not side swipe them with drugs. Drugs and alcohol make you vulnerable to the dark forces.

Jails are places were lost "birds of a feather" get together and reinforce their attitudes about social injustice, the "why me?" syndrome. What you are around and think about grows. Jails need reformative behavioral programs with specific techniques for individuals to understand, and take responsibility for their feelings, and actions. They need to know that how their feelings, and choices got them into jail. They need to know how to use their soul, to reprogram their choices.

What if these people had been taught to connect with God to get into altered states, and how to get into a meditation high? What if these people had learned that drugs were a bummer, and a rip off? What if these people had learned how to follow their heart and dreams as children, and follow their life love, and passion, with ongoing reassurances from God? How different their thoughts and realities would be if they were taught that there is a loving God available at all times to help guide our choices.

Learn how to do deep meditation or get hypnotized by a specialist. Learn how to love yourself, and what you are doing. DO NOT take drugs, or alcohol to cope, or socialize. God is the answer. God is the only way to freedom, for each individual's loving truth.

## MENTAL INSTITUTIONS:

What is insanity? Just like the people in jails, only 10 % are really and truly permanently damaged. When looking through various patients' charts, I found that what had happened to a person was insane, and they were reacting weird in response. We take these traumatized people, lock them up, and give them heavy doses of "intense" drugs to help control them. So you have overly sensitive, usually quite bright and somewhat psychic personalities, people who should never take drugs, on some aggressive and highly toxic chemicals with many side effects. After these individuals are totally drugged, you try to talk to them about their past. These individuals cannot believe where they are. The strange environment, the strange drugs can add such emotional abuse to an already unstable thought process. Many get so emotionally diseased by this hospitalization brain washing, and labeling process that they can never recover. In fact, our society says once you are labeled, that is it.

Mental institutions are filled with lost, lonely, meek people who do not know how to change their environments. They are souls in need of self-love. They must learn how, and where they belong. They need to know they had a temporary episode of ill feelings, but they can change, and be healthy and happy. It is normal to go through periods of mental anguish, trauma, and dramas. They do not know where they belong. God can tell them.

For example, if you are labeled bi-polar, then you will always be bi-polar. This is insane! It should say--- You had an episode of reacting to a situation that was manic-or depressive. So what? Learn about these energies, and use them. When you are feeling manic – GO RUN A MARATHON. Doubt you will still be manic! If you are feeling depressed there is usually a reason, so find out about it. Is it time to talk with your joy guide, and start some fun, and relaxing activities? How about dancing? How about music? SOUND THERAPY IS HEALING! ART THERAPY IS REAL. The universe has many modalities out there for all human energy systems to heal. Have you tried ALTERNATIVE CHINESE REMEDIES, VARIOUS MASSAGE MODALITIES, ART THERAPY, HYPNOTHERAPY? Find your inner guide, and find yourself. Fill your life with joyful, meaningful activities (energies). HAPPY PEOPLE ARE HEALTHY PEOPLE.

The truth about jails, mental institutions, and chronic care hospitalization units is that the people need hope and love to heal. They need to know that they had a bad episode that was insane. They need to know they can heal, that there is a way to change, heal, learn, and grow to be a good, healthy, happy person. They need to learn how to contribute to society, without hurting themselves or others. They need to learn how to cope differently with the energies they encounter, as well as with their feelings and reactions to various types of people. They need to learn how to find new activities, people, and relationships, to make healthy changes in situations and activities. When people can understand the power of their thoughts and feelings, they make new choices a reality. To understand a problem is the first step to changing the situation.

People must learn how to connect with their higher power. Hypnotherapy is like mental surgery. Hypnotherapy done with the right therapist can help a person remove blocks, and open a person to their higher power. These deep wounds need a type of mental surgery (hypnotherapy). These wounds are often buried so deep that the person does not even remember parts of the cause (not consciously.) These wounds have an emotional scaring. These adhesions must be cleaned out. The subconscious can be used to override the conscious waking state and change the person.

Dysfunctional parenting, combined with unruly hospitalization or institutionalization processes of containment and labeling are condemning--not healing. This emotional scaring causes others in our society to further label these people. In turn, these labels eat away at the self–esteem of that person. This is no way to help a person heal. They get worse, not better. When somebody gets emotionally ill, it is a reaction to what happened to him or her. This is reflected in the energy law of cause and effect.

They must know there is a way to heal. It is rarely a condition that is permanent. Past life work, with Spirit work, and dream work can truly heal these people. Why not try to heal these temporarily insane reactions to an abusive predicament? The situation was the cause of the effect for these individuals. They did not know how to deal with their situations and feelings "normally." What is normal? Who is judging whom?

It is known in our society, that any time you have low self-esteem issues you can easily end up using more drugs and/or alcohol. It is also proven that choices from thought patterns while under the influence of drugs or alcohol tend to be off balance. The more off balance the person is feeling, the more our society says have a drink or take a toke, or a smoke, or pop a pill, or eat, and or do one or more of the above in combination. Doesn't it seem obvious that the people who are abusing themselves or others are running from their fearful, negative, feelings? Anger and frustration come from deep wounds, lack of understanding, and limited coping mechanisms.

Emotional wounds affect the self-esteem. When people do not love themselves, they do not love others in a healthy manner. People who are wounded, and fearful, and do not know how to stop these feelings, bring on more worry and more negative situations (what you ponder will grow.) Is this insane or is this what they were taught? Or are people just reacting to bizarre situations because of their own chaos, lack of grounded lifestyle, and limited coping mechanisms? Are you a product from "The Quick Fix" Generation? What's with all the kids on ADD drugs? I have found these kids to be of a certain type of energy that needs lots of exercise, not drugs. I see the parents of most these kids as controlling. I see the energies of the child clashing with the parents, and the parents drugging their kids so they can cope around them, *their* way. How many ADD kids are put into a demanding or challenging sport? This energy is special to be used in a special way. God made everyone special, not sick. God can help you beyond any drugs!

Our Society is sick. Look at all the drugs out there on the market for depression, and social anxiety disorders. All the pills have serious physical side-effects. Pills do not heal emotional problems. By taking a pill you are admitting you have some kind of problem. The more you feel and think and decide you have a problem, yes, you will. What you put your intention on grows.

We have trained everyone to take something outside ourselves whenever we have a feeling that we do not like. Think about this: If you are ill at ease, before long you will be suffering from an illness. What do YOU take to feel better? Do you smoke, take drugs, alcohol, overeat, or take prescriptions? What about disease? What do YOU take if you are suffering from a disease? Chances are you go to a doctor when you are really ill. Chances are you will be given something (drugs) to get better. What about all the people, who self-medicate? They say they had a bad day, and must have a drink, or a toke, or a smoke. So many people have learned to self-medicate because doctors can be so very expensive or unavailable at night. This is just one part of the drug problem.

The next part of the drug problem has arisen from all the people who use Alcohol or Pot to socialize. We as a society have shown our adolescents they need to take drugs or alcohol to party. We have shown them they are not OK the way they are. We showed them that if you want to be comfortable at a party, or social place at night you need a drink, or glass of wine, or a toke of pot. The intentions behind the drugs are from teachings. The intention brings on the highs, not the drugs or alcohol. After, one or two drinks, other drugs become more enticing. Under the influence of drugs and alcohol is when choices become compromised, and unhealthy choices are made.

Choices made under the influence are NOT coming from the person's higher power. In fact, these choices are why we have to have more jails and hospitals for both physical and emotional chronic care. Isn't it time NOW for a change in our consciousness? Haven't enough problems arisen on this earth because of drug and alcohol use? It is time to re-evaluate our coping mechanisms as a human species. It is a known fact that methamphetamines, heroin, angel dust, ecstasy, cocaine, LSD are becoming more easily accessible to our youth. We must stop, and think about new choices. ALL HIGHS FROM ALL DRUGS ARE ALREADY IN YOU. Do not let someone rip you off from your God given abilities and Highs. How about a new fad? Let's start teaching how to MEDITATE instead of how to MEDICATE.

## FREE WILL Versus GOD'S WILL

Mankind has not changed since Adam and Eve decided to use their own ego-brain instead of listening to God. God is inside of each of us. It is time to remember our soul. We have a mind. Our mind is separate from our soul. It is time to learn how to reconnect with our divine guidance. Our soul is connected to our breath. Our Soul has Holy Spirits attached to it. These Holy Spirits are our divine guides. These divine guides are particles of our spirit. Everyone has his or her own unique spirit. How much is nature? How much is nurture? How much is our karma? How much is from our soul, from God?

All babies are cellularly the same. Every baby comes here unique. The mind and bodies tissues are the same. The difference is their spirit, their soul.

## THE MEANING OF YOUR LIFE, GOD KNOWS.

God knows the meaning of everyone's life. Your soul purpose, and the gifts you came to share are all inside your soul. With the help of trained spiritual guides, using meditation or hypnotherapy, you can learn to see, hear, talk, and feel, and know your spiritual guides. Everyone's spirit is attached to his or her soul. Everyone's soul is attached to God. Angels are near you. Angels can hear you. You are never alone.

This book is written to help people understand how to use the omniscient and omnipresent powers of the LOVE AND LIGHT ENERGY OF THIS UNIVERSE. We all are connected to it through our breath, our soul.

This book will help you understand how to use your soul connection to God. God is the only way to truth. God is the only way to freedom. God is the only way to true love of self, and for others.

Before you go much further, you may want to feel the universal life truths from the old hymnals. Holy spirits, and angels and visions are frequently talked about in all major religions and their hymnals. People have been inspired to write poetic truths about the Holy Spirits, Angels, The Light of God, and other Universal Spiritual Truths for centuries.

How did each of us get soooooo far away from God? We are so far from God! Too many people do not have faith, trust, belief, honor, or integrity in their lives. Too many people are living their lives far from love, far from their Godly truths. So many people are in fear, lack, pains (emotional, and physical), secrets, dramas and traumas. All people need to let go to God, and learn how God Can Help You!

# STUFFED FEELINGS=EATING DISORDERS, ADDICTIONS, INSANITY:

Feelings are human. All humans have feelings. We have both positive, and negative feelings. All feelings must be looked at. Why are you experiencing a feeling? There are many books out about feelings. It is time for each individual to examine his or her own feelings. Feelings are caused from a vibration. Many people talk about "vibes." Yes, it is time to take note of your own vibes about a situation, a person, a thought, a food source, or a thing. All vibrations are trying to tell each person something.

WHAT ARE YOU FEELING? What sense do you make of it? What is happening? Why are you feeling, what you are feeling? When in doubt, it is time to ask God. Usually, when humans start to doubt, and feel too many bad feelings they start to get sick from all the dis-ease they are taking in. The more you let your thoughts take hold of negative "vibes," the more energy you have going out to create more negative attitudes and behaviors. Thoughts are the beginning of actions, choices, behaviors, and habits.

Feelings are very important to understand. Each person has beliefs from their childhood nurturing process. BELIEFS will also affect your emotions, and reactions to certain stimuli. IT IS TRUE THAT EMOTIONS and BELIEFS are the cause of dis-eases of the mind, and body. The mind and body connection is a cause and effect mechanism that is responding to experiences from what it has seen, heard, touched, or tasted, or smelled before. All our cells are basically the same. All humans' brain tissues are basically the same.

There are obviously various genetic differences. All human tissue is the same. How our spirits act toward, and then respond to various stimuli, makes each of us different--yet similar. Feeling your vibes, and learning about how vibes interact with your choices, and thoughts is fascinating, and should be meditated on more.

Why are there about 200 emotions that all humans can relate to everywhere on this planet? Specifically, we have positive emotions, or feelings, and we have negative emotions or feelings. Life comes back to energy. There is a huge unlimited energy source we are not using, or rarely use. The basic of "good is good and bad is bad" seems to be universal. Why is there still so much bad energy, bad things happening on this planet? Is it just history repeating it self in the age-old quest of the "have and have-nots"? Why is there so much suffering? Is it because the people with power, and money are off-balance with their egos running wild, and reacting out of their own negative emotions and energy patterns?

Seems to me that some of the people in power are just children who were not brought up with love, and who were not taught forgiveness or how to share. Is the world suffering because of lack of love? How were you taught to behave and survive? Were you taught to harmonize with others, or just compete with others? How about forgiveness energy? How about the energy from Love vibrations? What were you taught about your feelings, and vibes? How different the world could be if people used their God energy like they use the Internet.

How different this planet would be if everyone knew how to share. There is enough money for all. How different this planet would be if all children knew they had a place and a reason to be alive, and knew how to use God's love energy, and that all the people they met were their brothers or sisters connected to the same God. How different this planet would be if everyone took responsibility for his or her own thoughts, and choices. How different this planet would be if all children learned how to go inside for direction, help and balance instead of going outside to some place or to some thing.

Seems to me, through my various studies with dreams, past life regressions, Holy Spirit work, Chakra work, dowsing, chi energy, light energy work, sound therapy, art therapy that the truth is, we are too far from God as individuals and as a world community. The only people truly happy and healthy are following their healthy passions in life. They have found a connection to an energy flow that is meaningful for them. These thoughts and driving energies come from their divine guidance, their inner knowingness, and passion.

Their true heart desire, true inspiration, comes from the word to inspire (comes from the breath). Again, we have come back to the most important human element: the breath. The breath is the way to inner peace. All yogis use meditation type breath work to increase flexibility of the physical plane. You only have about six minutes that you can hold your breath without having serious complications. Your spirit, your soul is connected to the breath.

Breathing has been used with all kinds of meditations. Meditation is a way of listening to God. All major religions, including Christianity, expound on the subject of meditation as a way to listen to God. All societies must learn how to MEDITATE, NOT MEDICATE. This process of learning how to reach for God instead of reach for a pill, a drink, a toke, or smoke, or more food will save the world. First it will help you save yourself. As you grow in spiritual knowledge, flow, and faith; and you trust in God to guide you, all your choices change. As your choices change, so do all your activities, friends, jobs, relationships, and life beliefs. What you thought was important, or hurting you, now is gone.

We are here to learn and grow. We are here to heal and help others heal. We are here to wake up to our soul purpose, and our gifts. Everyone has a heart dream. These deep heart dreams are always in the person's best interest, and never harmful, only helpful to others. Everyone has a reason to be here, everyone has gifts they came to share. Everyone must learn why he or she came and what each one has to share. When people are living with inspiration they do not want to hurt others.

We do create our lives by our choices. What you choose to do, what you choose to say, what you choose to eat, what you choose to drink, what you choose to be, what friends you choose, what activities you choose, what jobs you take, what beliefs you take, what organizations you belong to, what hobbies you choose, what place you decide to live, what clothes you decide to wear, what people you choose to talk with, what thoughts you choose to have. CHOICES, CHOICES, CHOICES!

Emotions are feelings from energy vibrations. There are too many people running around this planet off balance. If people are not using God in their lives daily, they are looking outside themselves to get balance, and help. When people are taking drugs or alcohol or smoking or over-eating to stop ill feelings, they have not dealt with the reality of why they are avoiding their feelings. People become more and more dependent on ways to avoid looking at their true feelings, they just want these feelings to go away.

Whatever people put their intent on grows then they start to get into habits that keep them caught in a certain pattern of choices. People are so afraid of change they tolerate bad situations. Fearful people start doing more bad habits to escape the growing fear. The more the mind stays attached to fear, the more fear can grow. Again, we are learning the power of our thoughts. NEWTON'S THIRD LAW OF PHYSICS=CAUSE AND EFFECT.

Our minds and bodies are not connected with our souls. Without having your soul connection you will inevitably end up emotionally or physically ill in your life. You will find life to be more depressing, full of fear, violence, lack, anxiety, suffering, pain, loneliness, greed if you only use your EGO mind and body for coping. The ego mind is very limited. It can only relate by what it has been taught. The ego mind also stores all wounds (just like other animals). So, if a child has had a lot of negative input (from TV, family dramas, negative parenting, or unhealthy peer pressure) he or she would in turn react as has been taught, or shown.

The cause and effect of lost unhappy, angry, unbalanced people is that they will raise other sick, unhappy unbalanced children. There is no real balance for any person's mind or body without the SOUL CONNECTION. HAPPY HEALTHY people are GROUNDED, and HAVE FAITH IN THEIR SOUL CONNECTION.

Everyone must learn the perfection of their soul connection to balance his or her particularly unique energies and talents God gave him or her. Everyone's unique talents, and soul purpose must be remembered to have a healthy mind, and body. Healthy individuals make healthy communities.

When people remember why they came, and follow THEIR DIVINE GUIDANCE they will find SELF LOVE. This is where true and grounded balance comes. When people learn to follow their DIVINE GUIDANCE they will find their SOUL MATES. WE HAVE SOUL MATES. This is the only way to find TRUE LOVE.

Learn how to love yourself, follow your path, and there will be your TRUE LOVE, a soul mate. Soul mates share the same values, heart dreams, and life goals. Soul Mates have the same energies mentally, physically, socially, financially, and spiritually and are on similar paths. Find yourself, find self-love, find your path, and then you'll find your soul mates. True lasting partnerships.

## MEDICAL HYPNOTHERAPY:

Science and medicine know there is more to life than meets the eye. There is another section of energy floating about called our subconscious. Scientists have known for years we are only using about 10% of our brain. Milton Erickson said, "Patients became patients because they were out of rapport with their own unconsciousness.... ...Patients are people who have had too much outside programming, and lost touch with their inner selves."

Medical Hypnotherapy is a state certified program to help people heal using subconscious connection to their mind and body. Medical Hypnotherapy can help people change and heal from a multitude of disorders. You can heal without drugs! I believe that drugs should be used for crisis intervention only. Crisis intervention drug therapies should only last 72 hours to maybe 2 weeks, ever! I have found that if you learn how to use medical, and spiritual hypnotherapy, you can keep your self in balance, and not go into horrible crisis situations.

Let it be known to mankind that people can change, and they can heal. First people must admit to a problem, believe they can change, and truly want to change. Medical Hypnotherapy can help alleviate, and heal all the following without drugs:

ALL TYPES OF ADDICTIONS
PAIN (especially the type from no known origin)
DEPRESSIONS all kinds
LOW-SELF ESTEEM
ADHD or ADD

ANXIETIES all kinds
PHOBIAS
POST TRAUMATIC STRESS DISORDERS
SOME TYPES OF CANCER
MANY MEDICAL DISORDERS
BURNS AND EMERGENCIES
PSYCHOSOMATIC DISORDERS, AUTOIMMUNE DISEASES, IBS, etc.
NUEROLOGICAL, AND OPHTHALMOLOGICAL CONDITIONS
SLEEP DISORDERS
ASTHMA, ALLERGIES, TINITUS, TOURETTES, DYSLEXIA, ENURESIS
SEVERLY DISTURBED PSYCHIATRIC DISORDERS
MULTIPLE PERSONALITY DISORDER
RELATIONSHIP PROBLEMS
SEXUAL PROBLEMS

Also Hypnotherapy can:
Help you have a beautiful, natural labor and delivery!
Help you enhance your academic, aesthetic, or athletic abilities!

The following information is from the American Society of Clinical Hypnosis.

> ➢ It is time to let people know they do not necessarily need to take a pill to help them heal. There are no known side effects. There are some myths, misconceptions, and fears about hypnosis.

- *Fear of revealing secrets-genuine concerns that they will tell all or reveal some secret from the past. In fact while hypnotized the subject has greater awareness than when fully awake and retains the power of selectivity.*

- *Myth of the weak mind-*there exists a belief that only the weak minded or gullible can be hypnotized. Actually it appears that it is quite different, and the opposite is in fact most likely true. People of above average intelligence who are capable of concentrating and those who have active, vivid imaginations make the best hypnotic subjects.

- *Fear of humiliation-*afraid they will be made to look or act like a fool. Something like what they saw on some stage show or movie. The stage show volunteers wanted to participate. These people wanted to act silly, and clown around. They were there by choice, and knew what they were doing.

- Fear of loss of control-*who would want to lose control? A hypnotized subject is in full control of their own self, fully aware of the environment, and completely capable of making decisions. If the subject were to be presented with an idea or suggestion they would find objectionable in regular consciousness, it would still be objectionable and would be rejected during hypnotherapy.*

- Fear of not waking up-*Hypnosis is not a sleep. There are many differences. The main difference is that during hypnosis you are in a heightened state of awareness. If you do fall*

> *asleep after becoming very relaxed, you will feel refreshed and have no ill effects at all.*

The Medical and Science Communities are learning more and more about the subconscious parts of the brain. Hypnotherapy, if done with the "right" therapist, can help you change your life. It is always important to feel the VIBES you get from any practitioner.

Everyone's energy is different. We are all made up of atoms. We all have our own unique spirit with our very own electromagnetic field about it. Music resonates differently for different people. These same types of vibrations come through different types of auras of different types of people. If you go to someone and you do not feel comfort--truly relaxing comfort from them--they may not be the best healer for you. You need to ask your higher power.

HIGHER POWER-oh yes! This is the beginning of the rest of this book. This information can help you learn HOW, WHY, AND WHEN TO TALK TO GOD and ways to hear, see, and feel God's vibrations (signs) for you.

# SPIRITUAL HYPNOTHERAPY:

This is so exciting! What an incredible time we live in. I want to talk to you about the connection of our subconscious mind with our soul. The Third eye, the chakras, the chi energy of acupuncture, and shiatsu are all a part of the physiology of the soul. There is an anatomy of the spirit. This is becoming the wave of the future. This electromagnetic field from our atomic structures helps a person to understand the physics of the relativity of matter, with quantum physics. This is where science and spirituality mesh. You can dowse the chakras with a pendulum, and actually feel open or closed areas. Similar to how people dowse for water. Chakras have real, measurable energies.

There is another type of Hypnotherapy that can truly evolve you to another level of joy, peace, love, so you can be a part of the light energy of God. God is all the love and light energy of the universe, not just planet earth. God is part of this anatomy of your spirit energy. You can learn how to ask the universal energy for help, and receive answers, by listening, dowsing, asking for signs, watching for the signs, and by paying attention to your dreams. You can do this by getting help with a past life expert who can take you into the light after the death cycle, and by a spiritual hypnotherapist who can help you learn to see, feel, and know your own Holy Spirits (angels, master teacher, joy guides, and wise ancestors).

SPIRITUAL HYPNOTHERAPY WILL HELP YOU! Spiritual hypnotherapy is a way to connect to your soul. Your soul is attached to God. Everyone can learn how to remember why they came, what gifts they have to share, and how to attain love, joy, and peace. God wants us to remember our soul, our true spirit. God wants everyone to help create heaven on earth. Only by changing yourself--finding yourself--can you show others the path to health and joy, love, peace, balance.

God gave you everything you need to have a good life here--but, but, but you must learn how to talk to God, feel God, hear God and see God's vision for you. YOU must let go of free will, and let God Help you. This universal law of our universe is so important. Your spirit guides are attached to your soul. They cannot override your free will. Learn how to ask for help, and listen for your guidance.

Remember earlier about Adam and Eve? FREE WILL is always there for you. Free will is attached to all those awful, and empty addictions. Free will won't give you unlimited healthy choices. Free will is attached to habits and limited to the ego-brain. The ego brain is very fearful, and stores all negative situations. The ego brain is very limited in its ability to make expanded choices. The ego brain is like a cold Yellow Page full of information. A situation arises, and the ego-brain reacts to the situation as it has a memory of teachings, and reactions of doing or saying something. The Course of Miracles, by the Foundation For Inner Peace refers to this separation of mind (ego), and spirit (soul) throughout its pages.

Even the Medical Hypnosis handbook from the American Society of Clinical Hypnosis Book indicates reference to a section of great inner importance. This section is called "Getting in touch with your inner advisor."

God is inside everyone. We have a choice to choose God's way or follow our free will. Free will leads people astray. Free will can lead you to an empty nothingness. Free will can get you committed to a mental hospital, free will can get you into a jail, free will can get you into lots of lust, free will can get you into a chronic care unit of a hospital, free will can get you into AIDS, free will can get you into endangering someone else's life. When you stop to think of it free will is ruining the world.

God does not want us to be unhappy. God wants our lives to shine. God wants everyone to wake up, and remember how to call on his love and light energy. God wants all people of all nations to remember their soul. People must learn how to use: their soul advisers, their God given divine guidance, their inner knowingness, their inner advisors.

The Bible has many wonderful teachings about visions, angels, and holy spirits. The Bible mentions visions, (and dreams) over 700 times. The Bible also talks of Angels, and Arch Angels, and Holy Spirits. Angels are mentioned over 200 times in the Bible. Our subconscious, again, is attached to the dream state. We will take some space here for people to learn that many dreams are coming from their higher power, God. We are not alone. We all have holy spirits attached to our breath. The free will is asleep when you sleep; so, the Holy Spirits can give you messages in your sleep.

# DREAMS

Dreams are important! Dreams are attached to our higher power. This higher power is trying to help guide you, help you to see, or feel something that you are not taking time to see or feel in your conscious state. Dreams can be a beacon to help you out of danger to safety. Drugs and alcohol affect the dream state. Whenever you choose outside of yourself for peace, and do not ask for God's help, your life can go off balance.

Dreams are there to help you solve problems. Thomas Edison, once said, "Ideas come from space." Ideas, solutions, and insights can come through in visions.

"Every major writer in the first four hundred centuries of Christianity regarded dreams as one way that God offered healing and guidance to mankind," says Reverend John Sanford, author of *Dreams: God's Forgotten Language*. This statement from Rev. John Sanford came from Wilda B. Tanner's book, *The Mystical Magical Marvelous World of Dreams*. There are some other wonderful books out about dreams. Denise Linn, and Betty Bethards also have books out on the significance of the various signs, and symbols that are given via the dream state to each individual to help them with their life challenges. Your angels can come to help you in your dream state because your free will is asleep. Remember you must ask for help from the universe so your angels can help give you guidance. The law of the universe is that Angels cannot override free will, but will help you when you sleep.

God knows all the meanings to every thought and dream you have. God is part of you. You can learn how to meditate on the meaning of your dreams. You can be hypnotized and get right back to the dream for deep understandings. You can also get several books from the authors I have mentioned and feel for the "ah-ha vibration" of inner truth. This means you can write down your symbols from dreams, and look up several options for their significances for you and feel for the correct "AH-HA" or the "Yes, that's it" feeling. This feeling can also be called "Lightbulb moment" or goosebumps.

Dream journals can be a fun way to help you with part of your soul connection work. As the Bible quote says, "without a vision the people perish." When people are not truly inspired by an inner dream, or vision, they seem to fall for other people's goals, and are subject to manipulation and disappointment.

"KNOW THAT I AM WITH YOU AND WILL KEEP YOU WHEREVER YOU GO."-Genesis 28:15

"How great are his signs, how mighty are his wonders."-Daniel 4:3

"I the Lord maketh myself known to them in visions; I speak to them in dreams."-Numbers: 5-6

HOLY SPIRITS ARE AROUND US. ANGELS CAN HEAR YOU. ANGELS ARE NEAR YOU. I will be sharing just a few of my clients' stories with you, to help the world know there is a God--WOW! YEA!

HOW YOU CAN CONNECT TO YOUR SOUL is a fantastic, exciting, fun, and exhilarating discovery to your true self. God has unlimited good tidings in store for you if you will let go of free will and ask to follow God's will.

# PART TWO

# TRUE CLIENT STORIES

These stories are true. The names have been changed to protect the client's privacy. I like to use two different questionnaires. Part of the Health questionnaire has a section about Medical-History. My Health questionnaire is followed by another Clinical Hypnotherapy questionnaire. With the help of these two case history questionnaires (one for the mind and the other for the body), I am able to understand what has been happening to this person here on this planet.

## Jamie's Story:

## BI-POLAR, SUICIDAL TEENAGER/ CLINICAL DEPRESSION

Jamie came from out of town with her Aunt Teresa on a vacation to the Gorge. They decided to come into my office for a couple of massages. Jamie's Aunt came in first. While Jamie waited in my waiting room she began to read about Hypnotherapy. By the time it was Jamie's turn for a massage, she decided she wanted to try this hypnotherapy instead.

Jamie had a history of being in and out of three expensive Psychiatric Hospitals. They had labeled her as a Manic-Depressive personality, with strong bi-polar tendencies. She had been put on four different drug regimes to manage her symptoms and behaviors. All these labels were not helping her to heal. These hospitals were telling her she was sick. The drugs' side effects made her more ill. She started to lose hope. She knew she was unhappy with her life. She knew she felt sick inside. The drugs and the tender loving care while in the hospital would help a bit to alleviate some of her depression and various mood swings.

But when she would get out of the hospital, and be alone with labels telling her she was sick, and must have a pill to feel better, she would take the pill and sometimes feel worse. She would take another, hoping to feel better. She was so lost.

Pills will not heal your life. Your feelings are with you for a reason.

If all you have is a pill to rely on, for your well-being, you are in deep trouble! All drugs will start to hinder the person, both physically and emotionally. This is when people tend to give up. This is when many become institutionalized. They feel the labels mean they are forever sick. When the pills do not work, they feel worse. What is the use? Is this it? Is this all I get? When all they know is a pill, or quick fix to let go, they really have no place to let go, and get help. The circle of pain becomes vicious, with scarier, deeper problems with deeper hurts, and more thoughts about all the pain.

Once sick, always sick? This is not true. No, no, no. God can heal anything physical or emotional. Everyone gets sick emotionally or physically on this earth plane. All illness comes from a lack of love. All illnesses can be healed through God, but can depend on Past Lives and Karma!

Jamie went into trance easily. She was seeking so desperately. She so needed help. God came for her. I was trying to control the session my way, for medical depression relief, when her DEAD FATHER showed up. I could feel a change in the room. She had told me that her life had gone down hill into deep depression when her father died in a tragic car wreck. She assured me she had gotten over it in the hospital.

Her father knew exactly what to say to help her. She had soft tears, and I could see her crying. I went over to the table to comfort her. She said her dad was going now, but not to worry because, he would introduce her to her Guardian Angel. It turned out that she had not finished grieving her dad's loss, and felt unsafe. As her Guardian Angel came near, I felt a warmth in the room, softness, and comfort that I could see come to Jamie. Her body seemed so tranquil, and she now had a soft loving smile on her face.

More soft tears came from Jamie's eyes. Jamie was in trance and talking to her Guardian Angel. Her Guardian Angel told her she was always by her side-- she did not need to be afraid, she did not need to hide. She would help her everyday to feel safe and comforted. All she needed to do was ask, then go into deep breathing, and then listen. She would always be able to help her stay safe. I heard and felt Jamie take a big breath, and let go.

Then, all of a sudden Jamie started to laugh. Jamie was laughing so hard she nearly rolled off the table while she was still in trance. I asked her what was going on? Jamie said, "Simon is here now. He is so funny, and cute. He has been with me seven lifetimes, and waiting for me to learn how to communicate with him. He is my JOY GUIDE. He tells me all I have to do whenever I am feeling depressed is to call on him. He will tell me what to do, or who to call, or where to go to put a smile on my face. I do not ever need to feel lonely or depressed again. He can always help me.

Anytime, anyplace, anywhere he is available for me. All I have to do is call his name, and ASK for help, and go into breath, and listen for his advice. He is part of my soul."

I then brought Jamie back to the room, and led her out of trance. She looked different than before. She had a more confident expression, and seemed more relaxed. I was so shocked by this whole experience. I could not believe what was happening. The words came to me, "Seek and ye shall find, knock and the doors will be opened."

A hymnal song became alive. It was called, "Work Wonders from Within" by Carmen Moshier:

Work wonders from within that's where to look, within.
There is no use looking somewhere else for powers that you need to win.
Work wonders from within; be sure you look within.
Just take your mind from outer fears; Don't think it's too late to begin!
In you, in me there's power to be.
In you in me, there's power that will set us free.
My course is up to me; Of course it's up to me!
So I'll set my mind to use my power if wonders I want to see!

What a day for me! I do not know who was more astounded Jamie, or I?

Now what was I to do? I did not want to take any classes on past lives. I knew this was a touchy subject for the masses. I was so hoping the Bible had sections on past lives. Other major religions had information about Past Lives. Buddhism, Hinduism, Native American Spirituality have strong beliefs about past lives. What was I getting into? My two older brothers were born again Christians. They were both openly upset with me. I tried to explain that this is God's work. I disbelieved a lot of what was happening myself.

I tried to keep my clients from going into to this type of trance area. I felt estranged, and a bit unnerved by this experience. The more I tried to control my clients' trance states the more HOLY SPIRITS KEPT COMING TO RESCUE THESE LOST SOULS. These Holy Spirits' love was extremely evident, as is, their knowingness for each client. Their information was always "right on" and from unconditional love.

By my willingness to help others heal, God came to help me. I started to go through all my own old beliefs. What was happening? Why was this happening? I knew it was my spiritual awakening process also. I felt in my heart God wanted me to remember all the lost souls that were misunderstood in the Psychiatric wards, the children suffering needlessly in the Pediatric wards of the chronic care units of the hospitals, and the poor lost souls that were in jail from using drugs, and alcohol. None of these people were happy the way they are. They all are lost. They all are trying to find a high, love, from outside themselves. They all gave their power away to the wrong people or substances. None of these people were happy. None of these people were living their lives with passion from divine inspiration. None of these souls knew of their God-given talents they were here to follow. None of these souls were connected to their inner higher power. They were all disconnected, looking to the wrong people, or some substance to make them feel OK.

**Claudia's Story:**

## LOOKING TO MEN FOR LOVE, FINDING DADDY ISSUES

One of my best friends was going through so many relationship problems. She was looking for love. She SO wanted a life partner. Claudia did not realize just how much she missed her dad growing up. She had deep-seated issues about not being good enough. She had deep rejection feelings and abandonment issues. She wanted her dad to care about her. She realized that her dad was a womanizer. He had been married seven times. He was always flirting around. He left her mom when she was a young child. She wanted his attention. This deep desire put signals out to the type of men that were also womanizers. She wanted her dad to spend time with her and adore her, so the universe brought men like her father to her.

Until Claudia could understand her feelings, she could not change her thoughts. She needed to honor who she was--put her heart's truth out to the universe. Concentrate her thoughts and feelings on how her life partner should be. She must understand to love her values, her heart interests, and life dreams first. Claudia needed to learn how to feel worthy to ask the universe to help her to get her true love. She must be whole unto herself and on good track to find another like her. If all she puts out is how she wants her dad to love her, then this focus of mind/thought vibration goes out to the universe, and she will get what she put time and attention on. What she wanted to have from her painful thoughts and feelings, the universe was trying to supply. More womanizers kept coming to her.

Thoughts and feelings help create your reality.

She tried all the "normal" counseling routes. After every appointment, she would come and let go to me. I said I could possibly help her. Why not try a session of Hypnotherapy. When two other counselors suggested drugs to help her, she knew in her heart it was time to try my work.

It took a while for her to relax and go into trance. She then opened up her heart chakra and asked for help. (I was trying to lead her with relationship scripting). I heard her say hello, and it was not to me. I asked her who was there with her. She said Jesus was there for her. He told her not to worry. He told her not to marry the man she was engaged to. He told her there would be another, to be patient. He told her that her other partner was getting ready for her. He told her he had issues he was working out. Jesus told her to pray, and listen for his guidance for her. Jesus told her to trust him. Claudia knew that Jesus had more understanding of her than any human being she had ever met. Jesus said he was always there to help her, anytime, anywhere.

Oh, Oh, now what am I going to tell people? How can I tell people that Jesus came to one of my clients? How can I tell people that Jesus cleared up my client's life in about 15 minutes? I was getting nervous.

I decided I needed help here. The more I asked for help the more I received. Because I was a member of the ABH (American Board of Hypnotherapy), I received ongoing information that this is a real healing gift. This is not weird. In fact, there are many others that are very aware of how soul work can heal your life. There are many people on this planet who are awaking to their God essence. Others are remembering their soul purpose, remembering their spirit, and how to use it to heal their lives. Others are talking about and using angel therapy. There are alchemists, talking about ascension and God energy. I found others who had been using Holy Spirits for inner guidance work also.

Doreen Virtue, PhD had a big impact on my life. I was in transitional period of my life when I decided to go to one of her workshops. Doreen Virtue PhD has several books: *The Lightworkers Way, Angel Therapy,* and *Divine Guidance.* These three books helped me understand my gift. She gives in-depth knowledge about angels, and spirit guides, and Master Teachers. She helped me with my work. She knew of my gift, more than I did. My significant other was present that day also. We both bought all her books. We had such an enlightening day. I started to remember my childhood. I remembered I came here to help heal people so they, in turn, would help save the earth.

Why were religions allowed to fight with armed weaponry? Promoting war, not Love. When children are taught Love, they do not want to hurt others. Religions must change! The religions must teach sharing, and caring, and do unto others as you wish they would do unto you! There is enough for all if we could learn how to share, not use fear and might. No mothers want to have their children go to war. We need to have more women run the world, to help it heal. Stop putting any savior above another savior. Savior worship only causes more separation, and discernment. They all came to teach love, and God realization in each and everyone alive. Spirituality is not about a savior, or a specific master teacher, it is about your God energy inside of you. True spirituality is how you work with God in your life. Spirituality is about your choices—your work, your words, your actions—not about some saviors. We all are brothers, and sisters connected to the same God; we all are alive for a healthy reason, if we choose to remember and use God daily.

We must have our breath. Our breath is our connection to God. Our individual spirits are all connected to our individual souls. We all have eternal souls. We must remember we will get what we give, so give Love. Give Love to yourself, and others. Isn't Love what you want?

What good is war when we have the ability to destroy our earth? Why were people making war, allowing religions to fight? Why weren't the Religions teaching people to love themselves, and others? Who was teaching Love? Where is Love? How do you find Love?

The more I looked for teachers, and confirmation to my knowingness deep inside my soul, the more information and teachers arrived into my life. "ASK AND YE SHALL RECEIVE." After getting my RN LICENSE and working in rural Oregon, and then in a remote area of Canada I gained more and more information as to why illnesses, and diseases, and even accidents happened to people. EVERYTHING HAPPENED FOR A REASON.

Louise L. Hay is another wonderful teacher. She has Hay House, Inc. One of her books, *You Can Heal Your Life,* came just when I needed it, from a friend I also needed so much! I was so glad to see this information that confirmed all of my inner knowingness about diseases, illnesses, and accidents in a written form. I had seen and experienced so many of her concepts while becoming an RN in the U.S. and in Canada. She writes with clarity and truths. She brings out quite specifically how different emotions cause different body ailments. How your thoughts and feelings affect your body.

Another teacher of mine was Betty Bethards, (she has an entire inner peace foundation). She also knew, years ago, about drugs. She knew Drugs would not heal a person. She knew that all the "highs" from drugs are already inside of each person. She started a program, MEDITATION: TURN ON, WITHOUT DRUGS. God can take you higher than any man-made drug. God can do more for you than any kind of drug.

Marianne Williamson is another speaker and author whose life is devoted to helping people get in touch with God. There are many more. It is time on this earth to learn how to choose the light and love of God. "Then an angel of the Lord stood before them, and the glory of the Lord shone around them." –Luke 2:9

So many were aware of this energy of love and light centuries ago. Look into the Bible with your heart open. Look for all the references in the Bible that speak of about the light of God. How about the Torah? How about the Kabala? How about Buddhism? All the Holy masters taught the same. Stop hiding behind some book, some savior, some priest, and some one outside of your self. Take responsibility to learn how to love yourself. Find out why you are here, and feel your feelings.

So many of my clients speak of this light they see, and feel and become a part of in trance. Go take a closer look through the hymnals for all the references to Angels, Holy Spirits, the light of God, Love, Joy, and Dreams. Love, light of God, and Holy Spirits, are all here for all of us the same way, inside as part of our soul. As you become happier you bring to yourself happier people. Like begets like.

**Karen's Story:**

## DEGENERATIVE ARTHRITIS, PAIN PILL ADDICTION

Patti brought Karen in for a session with me. Karen was so sick. Karen's friend knew I would not judge her; I would try to help her. Her life had become so painful. She had spent years getting sick so her mother would pay attention to her. The only time her mother was nice to her was when she was sick. Her mother had died. She felt responsible. She also felt guilty about feeling relieved. She had so many conflicting emotions that she became very upset. She started to take more and more medication to relieve her painful emotions.

She wanted to relax, and she wanted to relieve the pain she was experiencing. The only way she knew was to take something. She also started to drink with the medicine. She looked so awful. I could hardly recognize her. MY heart wept. I prayed to God to help me help her. It worked. God works.

She went into trance quite quickly, she so needed help. Her DEAD MOTHER showed up. Her mother finally understood the pain she allowed her daughter to go through, and her mother asked for her forgiveness. Her mother was sorry for her own life. Karen could see her mother's own shortcomings, and misery. Karen understood that her mother wanted her to have a better life now. As Karen let go, and could forgive her Mom, for all the hurt she inflicted emotionally, Karen was made free of this old hurting energy bond. They both made efforts toward reconciliation and love.

I felt movement in the room. Soft sweet smells came floating forth. Karen was starting to look young again. She looked so much healthier. All of a sudden, I could see she was talking to someone. I asked her who was there now. She said it was Joseph. Joseph was there for her. He told her she was safe now. He told her not to be afraid. He wore a five-point star on a brown robe. The star was to symbolize to Karen to remember to follow her own light within. Joseph told her he was always there for her, to help light her way. Joseph could help her to stay calm, safe, and be strong.

There was another shift in the energy of the room. This time Karen started to make soft murmuring sounds. I asked, "What was going on now?" Karen said that Raphael was there. Raphael was there to help her joint disease heal. He took his green light into her diseased body to help the cells heal. Raphael is an Archangel of God. His angelic color is green. God can heal through Raphael. Raphael can also help people release all their fears to have more faith in God.

Raphael also told her to have sound therapy every day to help her cells heal. Spend more time with music around her daily.

God was there via these guides, to help her with all her major life challenges, and struggles. I just let go and allowed God to work with her. All the while I wondered, why me? Why is this happening? What is going on with my work? Man, oh man, I felt honored, yet apprehensive; anxious, and a bit terrified. What was I doing? I knew people did not want to accept Medical Hypnotherapy, how on earth was I going to talk about Spiritual Hypnotherapy? Why me? Don Walsch's book came to mind <u>Conversations with God.</u> God had spoken to Don Walsch, why not to my clients? We all are supposed to talk to God ourselves. Actually, the more you listen to God's will the better your entire life will become. So, here I was learning daily about spirituality and soul guides.

I started to feel that I was ready to go through more spiritual awaking myself. I had to honor the fact that I came here to help people. I had to remember what I was told. I was told I must help the meek inherit this world. I was told to have trust in my divine guidance, and not to worry so much. I was told Emmanuel was with me. I was told Peter was with me. I was told to have trust, and faith in God. I was told I did not need to use drugs or alcohol, or to stuff my feelings. I was told to learn how to use my soul connections to the infinite higher power of the universe that is full of Love, and Light, and Holy Spirits waiting for us to get to know them, and use them. I was told to give Love and Light to the world.

I did not understand the words soul, spirit, faith, trust, God, or any of the Bible just three years ago. I did not believe in a higher power. I did not believe in any religious traditions. I was beginning to feel why Doreen Virtue, Ph.D said I was a Great, Great Priestess. I was so honored, yet dumbfounded by her statement. Her statement seemed so off track. Her statement seemed so weird, yet parts of me, understood.

Even as I write, I know God is the only answer to everyone's health, joy, and abundance. All major religions talk about Higher Power. You can read about it, or hear about it at worldwide worship "religious" gatherings. Yet, the truth lies within. This divinity of unlimited potential is inside each of us. We have free will to choose to use our higher power, or not to use it.

Even a few years ago, I could not have believed any of this myself. The messages from the Native American culture, the Kabala, the Torah, the messages from Bahai's teachings, Buddhism, the Bible and other ancient Hymnals are ALL coming to life for me. A bit different in words, a bit different in times, a bit different were the historians; yet, all the messages are so similar. There is a HIGHER POWER.

**Fred's Story:**

## CHEWING TOBACCO, SMOKING, AND MAKING AND USING 'METH'(SPEED)

Fred came to quit chewing tobacco and smoking. He had been so involved in drugs. He had been busted and gone to jail. He was trying to recover from making, selling, and using metheamphetamines. He looked so old, for only being 27. He seemed sincere to get help.

He went into trance quickly and found himself with a spirit guide. Her name was Cleops, his guardian Angel. He asked her for help and a big circle of light came to him. One half of the circle was white, and the other half was black. He asked the circle to come closer. He asked for help and guidance. Jesus came out of the circle from the light. Satan came out of the circle of blackness. Jesus went to some others of light off in the distance. Jesus was doing a circle dance. Fred asked Jesus for help. Jesus said you have free will. Satan is attached to your free will. Jesus told Fred his lessons of this life are to rebuke the darkness, and trust in the light, and learn to overcome his ambiguity. Jesus told him to give himself fully to love.

Fred asked Jesus for a sign of a gift. Fred wondered if he had a gift he could share to make money on this earth plane. Fred felt God might not want to help him because of his past. Fred asked for forgiveness, and asked for help. Fred knew he needed to know a better path, a better way of life.

He saw a sword with a noticeable double edge. Fred was so aware of the duality he was in because of his drug dealing. The sword can also mean the slaying of the ego, and cutting through the veil of illusion of life. Fred also saw the sword circling around a rose. This red rose had a yellow and white light coming out of it. The rose is a universal sign of love and beauty, and in some cultures it is the mystic center of the heart. The yellow was about his inner wisdom. The bright light is about the light of God coming forth from his heart, and his inner wisdom.

The sword kept clearing the aura around his heart to keep him closer to God. Also, Fred was to remember to choose the right side of life. When the darkness is getting too close Fred had a sword to cut off the dark energy. He had to use his courage to cut off all the ties with the dark druggies.

When Fred seemed to understand these messages from Jesus, then Cleops reappeared to him. She went to one side of Fred, and Jesus also reappeared on the other side. They both took Fred by each arm, and started to pull him off the ground up into the sky. He was floating upwards into a dark tunnel. At this time, Fred also needed to hang on to Jesus and Cleops. This tunnel was long and very dark with many doors on each side. All the doors he saw open at this time were dark. The only light was at the end of the tunnel, but this door was closed. Fred had let go of Jesus, and was only being led by his Guardian Angel Cleops at this time.

Fred so wanted to go into the room with the light. He kept pushing, and trying to get in. I was able to tell him you must ask from an open loving heart to get in. He sincerely tried, and then the door opened. Fred went into the light of God. He felt so relieved. He felt the unconditional love, and comfort. Fred knew beyond any doubts, that this is where he could find all his answers for his life. God was there for him. He also knew that anytime, anywhere he could talk to Jesus, and Cleops. Both Jesus and Cleops would be there for him, and now he could hear their voices. Fred learned how to pray, and go into breath, and to meditate (LISTEN TO HIS SPIRIT GUIDES). The only way through Fred's darkness would be to follow, and hold onto, the direction of Jesus, and Cleops.

"Call to me and I will answer you, and will tell you great and hidden things that you have not known."
     -Jeremiah 33:3

"Be strong, and let your heart take courage, all you who wait for the lord "-Psalm 31:24

"Trust in the lord with all your heart."-Proverbs 3:5

"Everything old has passed away; see, everything has become new."-Corinthians 5:17

"Do not be conformed to this world, but be transformed by the renewing of your minds so that you may discern what is the will of God-what is good acceptable and perfect"-Romans 12:2

"I intend to keep on reminding you of these things, though you know them already, and are established in the truth that has come to you. I think it right to refresh your memory."-2 Peter 1:12-13

# PAST LIVES............Oh, Yeah!

PAST LIVES must be addressed in this book. For some reason, Christianity took the information about past lives out of the Bible. I believe I heard it was in 600A.D. I have heard some say, that it is due to the fact that Christians want people to be more responsible for this life now. However, our souls are eternal, and God's energy is unlimited, and infinite. By now, I had nearly 10 people talk with Jesus during a session. Jesus knew exactly what each client needed. I had several guardian Angels, other ancestors, joy guides, helper angels, other religious masters, deceased family members, and various Saints come to various clients during their session. I do not know who is more excited about working with Holy spirits--my clients who get to actually see them, and talk to them--or me, while I watch and feel the energy shifts, and get to help guide these clients on their Journey. I feel so blessed to be a servant for God, to help people wake up to their true nature, which is divine.

There are past lives. There is Karma. Other major religions know more about reincarnation than Christians do. It is important to know that you will get whatever you give. If you give too much darkness you will go to hell, if not in this life, in another one. I have found ineluctable evidence about Past Life work. I feel compelled to let people know what my clients have experienced, and let people know what God has told, and shown to me. Our souls are eternal. We have many lives and many lessons. Small children who die can come back. Our souls are not finite. Christians must know we have many lives, and chances to know God here on earth. Some souls go to a place that is hell to suffer until they truly repent. What you give you will get. THAT IS WHY IT IS SO IMPORTANT TO LEARN TO DO UNTO OTHERS AS YOU WOULD WANT THEM TO DO UNTO YOU.

We humans are here for a variety of reasons. We are in different stages of soul evolution. We all are living out many karmic cycles. Everyone's journey is different. Everyone has lessons and challenges to learn. Everyone has lessons they must learn to grow back to spirit. The more you can understand your soul, the more fulfilling your life will be.

Past life regressions can help you understand the lessons you are now facing. There are many reasons to find someone whom you are very comfortable with, who is a Certified Hypnotherapist, CHt. Find out if this CHt. specializes in Past lives. These therapists can guide you back to a life where the lessons are similar to those you are in now. Also, it is very important to know if your therapist will take you through the death cycle to the light. All the messages must be received and acknowledged in the presence of the light of God. Otherwise, the past life experience might not have much of an impact. Going through the death cycle is illuminating, and helpful for major life transitions.

Please note: only three years ago, I was not going to ever use past life work for any type of healing work. I myself found it to be weird. I had a near death experience that changed my life. All my beliefs, and all my priorities were changed. The minute I stepped into the light, I knew my life was to change.

I begged God to come back, because I knew my kids would not understand all my painful lessons. I came back to help heal all my life's abuse that I had tolerated because of fear. I came back to help others see, feel, know, and hear their own connection to God. I came back to help people who are suffering, so they can find a better way to live their lives. I came back to show there is hope, joy, abundance, and healing love when you choose God first. I came back to let people know how to let go to God, and let God (your divine Holy Spirits) guide your way.

I came back to help prove there is a God. I came back to help all people in all religions know God is inside of you. God is not in a book, not in a church, not through a priest, not through a savior, BUT right inside of you! God is always with you, for you, to help you know to save yourself. We are all brothers and sisters on this little planet, who must learn to share and care for each other. Everyone must learn how to talk to God. Everyone must learn how to pray, to breathe properly, to listen (meditate) on God's guidance, anytime, anywhere. We are all put here for a reason. Only God knows what is best for each person, our best and highest good. Again, we all have a soul. We all have a specific purpose, and specific gifts we came to share. All our needs, and our health and well being will only come when you allow God to help guide your day, in each and everyway.

Another reason for studying Past lives, was because all the Holy Spirits that started to come while my clients were in trance started to tell my clients about how many lives they had been with them. These Holy Spirits would proceed to explain to my clients about all these different lives they had lived with my clients, and how happy they were to finally get my clients to acknowledge them. I know this may seem a bit precarious to you, yet it is the truth. There are many other books, and religions and scholars that will testify to past lives.

To get the most out of a past life experience, it is important that you find the right therapist to make you feel comfortable. Also, make sure they are a Certified Hypnotherapist, CHt and have a loving heart. Lastly, make sure they will take you into the light after the death experience so you may ask God the truth about what you needed to learn.

**Panu's Story:**

## PAST LIFE EXPERIENCE

A young woman, white Caucasian and Japanese mix, came in to do a newspaper article about past lives. Her religious background—Buddhism—made her aware of the reincarnation process of the soul's eternal journey. She wanted to try a past life regression. She was hoping to better understand her family's religious background. Various cultures--Japanese, Chinese, Native Americans, and Hindus—all believe in past lives. They know our souls are eternal. They honor studies about reincarnation.

She was struggling with her young womanhood, and her fights with her parents about what she should, and should not do. The fights were affecting her deeply. She went into trance and found herself to be an African American boy. She was a boy child who kept running off into the street to play with his friends. She was a boy child in a big city--New York. This boy child would not listen to his parent's guidance.

Her parents, in this past life, repeatedly told her not to play in the street during a certain time of the day, it was too dangerous. She watched herself, as this boy child, get hit by a car, and killed. Her mother came out screaming, devastated. As this boy child, she felt this wonderful light energy come and put many arms around her and carry this boy body into the light. She saw this boy body, and knew it was hers. She knew then she was in the light of God. She felt weightless and so comforted. She asked what her lesson was, and was told, "You are to learn to respect your loving parents' advice."

This session deeply changed how she related to her parents in this life. She realized that her parents did truly love her, and wanted the best for her. She could see that her lesson was to understand her parents, and respect their advice for her. This was her lesson for now, just for her. This helped her change how she reacted to her parents' advice. This change in cause and effect made major choice changes for her life direction.

The light of God has all knowingness. Each person's life lessons are unique unto them. Their soul is unique. All babies are SO individual, why? They are so new, and all made of the same cellular tissue. All kids from the same nurturing family still turn out so different. WHY? The infinite soul of each child has its own lessons to learn. I feel it is not just with nature or nurture alone, but also about the spirit of the child. The more each child is allowed to be themselves, and loved the way they are, the happier and healthier they become as adults. The more children can stay connected to their spirit (heart felt dreams--the reason they came) the healthier the adult.

When parents have been brought up around negative behaviors, unbalanced, unloving coping mechanisms, there is a lot of fearful, darkness in this type of parenting. If parents have not learned how to love themselves, and understand themselves, how can they teach what they do not know? When parents are lost, and do not know the way, they extend more confusion, and more fear. It's the only thing they know. This is what they were taught, and so this is how they teach their children. The finite brain is limited. MONKEYS SEE, MONKEYS HEAR, MONKEYS DO.

Studying Dreams, and past lives, and getting in touch with divine guidance everyday is the way to remember your spirit. This is the way to love you. This is the only way to find your true path.

The healing experience can be remarkable. There are certain medical conditions, both physical and emotional, that can be healed immediately through the light of God. Everyone who has had an NDE-NEAR DEATH EXPERIENCE-can tell you the life altering enhancer it can be. Past Life regressions done properly, can also have this same effect. When Past Life regressions are done, and the client is taken into the light of God after the death has occurred, that client will forever change his / her life. When Past Life regressions are done with the right person, the client's experience can be more profound than an NDE.

Please take time here to do some of your own soul searching. What about all the references to Love, and the Light of God? All through the Bible there is mention that God is Love and God is light. All major religions worship this energy that is God. All the great spiritual hymns throughout the world have messages about this energy.

"For with you is the fountain of life; in your light we see light."-Psalm 36:9

Prayer for Protection by James Dillet Freeman from a hymnal: *The light of God surrounds you; the love of God enfolds you; the power of God protects you The presence of God watches over you. Where ever you are God is!*

Spiritual Hypnotherapy can help you connect to your soul, to your love and light energy that is part of your every breath. God is LOVE AND LIGHT. The more people try to understand their own connection to God the better their life will become. Choose God first.

If you are unhappy and unhealthy God can help you heal. The agony of change is the fear of the unknown. It has been so long since humans let go of their ego minds and listened to God daily. Once a week at church is not enough. God wants everyone to listen to his or her divine guides daily, anytime, anywhere. God wants people to remember how to talk to their Holy Spirits, and listen to their advice. We have been on such a one-way road, following our fearful, reactive ego brains for so long. We have been using destructive coping mechanisms for so long. We turn to drugs and/or alcohol for emotional, and physical comfort or to escape our problems. We turn to drugs and alcohol to party. What happened to us? Can we not play without drugs and alcohol? God said not to go outside you for true fulfillment. God is part of you.

## HOLY SPIRITS:

HOLY SPIRITS are available to us. There will be more client stories to help you understand how to use your Holy Spirits for healthy, choices instead of drugs, and or alcohol. There are many Holy Spirits available to us throughout our lives. We all have a Guardian Angel, just like the Bible says. We also have other specific angels we can call on for help. Our Guardian Angel is for when you are not feeling safe. She can tell you to call the police, or 911, or yell help, or yell fire, or call a friend, etc.

There is more fear, chaos, and complexity to our daily lives. Guns, fear, chaos, depression and drugs, and alcohol are a deadly mix--an explosion waiting to happen. There is only one way to let go of fear, and that is to give it to God. God can handle it, and explain how to use the energy for constructive projects and helpful behaviors. The energy and vibrations of fear must be felt and understood in order to change them. God knows how to help each individual with any emotion of any kind, especially the negative vibrations, and feelings. God can change fear to understanding and then to love. God knows what's best for you! Each person must remind one another to make sure God is asked into your problem, so God can help your situation. Ask your neighbor, "Have you checked in with God about your situation? Have you asked God for guidance? What did God tell you to do? Are you following God's divine guidance through your challenge?"

We have angels, and archangels, that want to help us. We all have a Joy Guide to help us have more fun.

When was the last time you asked God to help you play or have fun? Yes, God can help you to have fun! God wants the humans to be happy. We each have our own Joy Guide that is waiting to help us anytime, any day to put a smile on our face. We must ask for help, or else our Joy Guide cannot over ride free will.

If you feel sad, or blue, and do not know what to do, ask your Joy guide for help, and listen. If you are feeling lonely or depressed, try to discover what your Joy guide's name is, and call on him/or her for help to cheer you up. These spirit guides have been with you many different lives, and are connected to your soul, your breath. These guides are always with you and know you better than any other physical human being. They are part of your infinite soul, your spirit. Again, these spirits have been with you far longer than any other human being; so of coarse, they know how to help you better than your best friend. They know your past, and can see into your future.

These Holy Spirits are the ones mentioned in the Bible. LOOK THROUGH THE BIBLE FOR ALL THE WAYS THE HOLY SPIRITS ARE MENTIONED. Also, look through all religions about their spiritual messages from various spiritual guides. This is where the Bible talks about divine guidance. This is what the inner divine guidance is talking about. HOW ABOUT SOME OF THE HYMNALS? I love these three hymns in particular: "Holy Spirit, Source of Gladness," "Holy Spirit Truth Divine," and "Holy Spirit Ignite Each Heart." I can feel how they expound on the essence of our soul connection with Holy Spirits. These are just three of the wonderful old hymns that talk about the Divine Guidance from the

Holy Spirits that are available to us. The Following songs are from the HYMNAL, *WINGS OF SONG,* from the Unity Church.

"Holy Spirit, Truth Divine," by J.P. White (Samuel Longfellow, adapted)

Holy Spirit, Truth divine, Dawn up on this soul of mine; word of God and inward light,
Wake my spirit, clear my sight.

Holy Spirit, Love divine, glow with in this heart of mine; Kindle every high desire, Cleansing self in Thy pure fire

Holy Spirit, Power divine, fill and nerve this will of mine Be my law, and I shall be Firmly bound, yet ever free

"And the disciples were filled with joy and with the Holy Spirit."- Acts 13:52

## TRUE CLIENT STORIES

### Sue's Story:

## SUFFERING FROM OSTEOARTHRITIS, AND RHUEMATOID ARTHRITIS, OVER WT., PSORIASIS, AND VERTIGO.

Sue came in looking for a way to stop overeating. She wanted help to lose weight. Her entire body was a mess. She admitted to having enough drugs at home to fill a small pharmacy. She was taking a drug for all kinds of symptoms, and symptoms from side effects, and weird drug interactions. She had to have her gallbladder out, from too many drugs that destroyed it. She had to have a hysterectomy, and a bladder sling, and an intestinal bypass done.

Her body was a mess. Her body was a reflection of all her fearful, negative self worth feelings and emotions she had experienced over the years that had been stuffed and never dealt with them. Her deep emotional problems had upset her entire cellular chemistry, and instead of trying to fix it naturally, she took all kinds of pharmaceutical drugs that were no longer working. She had somehow been on an antibiotic every day for years. She thought she had to have it to keep her complexion smooth.

The list of her medications was astounding. How could anyone be on so many medications? Western Medicine's pharmaceuticals and Hospitals are good for crisis intervention only! Not for daily use! No one person is the same. To be on more than one or two Western drugs for more than 2-3 weeks daily is crazy.

Everyone reacts differently to drugs. Drug doses are unpredictable. Everyone has a different intake and metabolism of food, drink, and drugs. Everyone should talk to a pharmacist just as much as to a Doctor about all the different medications, and particulars about diet.

DOCTOR'S ARE NOT PHARMACISTS, NOR ARE PHARMACISTS NUTRITIONAL DIETICIANS. All Medications can have adverse food interactions. All Medications SHOULD SAY: THERE WILL BE SERIOUS SIDE EFFECTS, AND THEY ARE UNIQUE AS TO YOUR DIET AND EXERCISE-THIS MEANS PROBABLE DISATER IF TAKEN LONGER THAN 72 hours, and not longer than 2-3 weeks, MAX.

Humans do not need to get themselves into a medical crisis that lasts longer than 2-3 weeks. Go get alternative Health care. What is life without health?

Sue's organs were being abused from all the medications she was on. Sue had nowhere to go. Drugs were not helping her to feel better anymore. She truly needed help. First she needed to know that ALL ILLNESSES ARE FROM BEING ILL AT EASE, AND ALL DISEASE WAS FROM DIS-EASE. Which means a person is not in balance, that they are having a lot of "UNEASY FEELINGS." Feelings, as mentioned before, are vibrations of moods within and around us. We are energy masses. When our body systems have a lot of love around them, and are in flow, HAPPY IS HEALTHY!

When a person is very happy, and in flow they rarely get sick. Most every chronic illness comes from lack of self-understanding, or lack of self-love. The body stays out of balance (or ill at ease for too long, and major body dynamics come into play.)

The side effects from all the medications were further destroying her muscle tissue, blood, lymphatic system, and bone tissue. Our perfect natural bodies were not made to take a lot of weird chemicals for prolonged lengths of time. She also had become addicted to Valium (to help her from feeling ill at ease). As her emotional addiction grew so did her body pains. They were taking up all her thoughts. The more she disliked how she felt, the more pills she would take to stop or change the feelings and thoughts about herself. The more she tried to "drug" her feelings away, the worse she became. She was so far from herself, she could not get fulfillment anymore. She knew she must learn a new way to feel her feelings, and honor them, by learning how to take loving care of herself.

Sue knew her major problems were: worry from all her body problems, not being able to relax, feeling fat, various fears, wanting to deaden her senses, refusing to accept responsibility for her own feelings (victim role, and blaming others), NOT LETTING GO OF THAT WHICH IS OVER, easily irritated, deep criticism of authority, and feeling very put upon, a bit of desire to feel punished. She hated the feelings she had about her own mother. She did not know how to change these relationship energy bonds.

She went ahead and told me about the dream she had the night before she came in. It was so perfect. It was about herself, with a sister, and a sister-in-law, who were together in a motel and were buying new clothes. Sue realized that the clothes were about her outer appearance. How she looked to others on the outside. How she was feeling abut herself and others on the inside was very different. The attitudes and type casting of others by what they wear. Clothing can also signify different types of situations you are in and what you are doing with your time.

New clothing dreams can most definitely be a sign about new attitudes you need to take on, and wear for your own personnel growth. Sue was aware how significant this dream was when she admitted that she told people she had another doctor's appointment. She could not tell people that she was coming to a hypnotherapist for help with an addiction disorder. She could not even admit to the various addictions she really had. Sue's unconscious brain knew she needed help with more than some 20 extra lbs.

Sue knew in her heart that she wanted to get help to heal, not just take more drugs. She did not want any more surgeries, either. She realized how deeply she needed a new change (clothing change); that was truly different. She felt after hearing there were no bad side effects to hypnotherapy that she had nothing to lose. She had a lot to win. Why not try hypnotherapy?

Sue went into trance quickly. She went to her sacred place, and saw God there. I helped her open her heart, relax to let God know everything she felt, and to let go of her issues to God, so he could then help her. She talked and talked to God about her life issues. She was only comfortable sharing a few messages with me.

God told Sue, "You must learn how to help yourself." "You must try to let go of all the pills; especially, the ones that were no longer necessary, and hurting you physically, and emotionally." God told her to try and he would be there every step of the way. He told her to try, and that she can do it. Help yourself! God told Sue that her husband, and children, and especially the grandchildren would be there for her, also. They all would like to see her happy and healthy again.

God told her to do more water aerobics, and boating, and much more dancing. Sue and her husband loved to dance. They quit some years ago. Since she fell sick, nearly 12 years ago they have not done much at all for enjoyment together. Sue recognized the old clothes, the old patterns of daily living to be all about who was feeling sick that day. The more they feared and let their lives revolve around being sick, the more illness they experienced. AGAIN, THE PHENOMENA OF CAUSE AND EFFECT—WHAT YOU THINK ABOUT GROWS, and can BECOME YOUR REALITY.

God also told Sue to relax, so her husband would be able to relax. Sue had no idea that their energy as a couple was causing both of them such disease. Now it was up to Sue. Would she wear her new clothing? Would she learn from what she experienced in today's session? Would she try to help herself by asking for God's direction for her instead of popping a pill? Would she have faith in God? Would she listen to God? Would she ask for God's guidance? Would she trust God's guidance? This is the way she had to help herself, but would she? Free will is always there, and choices, choices, choices are ours. Spiritual hypnotherapy and meditation will help you to make the best choice for healthy changes, new attitudes. It reminds me of a T- shirt I once saw with the logo

"ATTITUDE IS EVERYTHING." Fearful ego choices are limited to societies coping methods (take something) to feel better. What about using one's soul to help?

"Listen, children, to a father's instruction, and be attentive, that you may gain insight."-Proverbs 4:1

"The lord will guide you continually."-Isaiah 58:11

"If we live by the spirit, let us also be guided by the spirit."-Galatians 5:25

"But you are not in the flesh: you are in the spirit, since the spirit of God dwells in you."-Romans 8:9

"I will counsel you with my eye upon you."-Psalm 32:8

THE HOLY SPIRITS ARE CONNECTED TO OUR SOUL, OUR BREATH. As long as we are breathing we can call on these Holy Spirits to help us in so many ways. As mentioned before, we have at least one Guardian Angel to help keep us safe. We also have a Joy guide in times of sadness. VERY, VERY IMPORTANTLY, WE HAVE A MASTER TEACHER. We all have a master teacher available for life questions, our big life challenges, and struggles. Our Master Teacher may not be Jesus. Jesus was one of God's chosen sons. He was the only way to the light, and the truth, while he was alive. His teachings are about finding your way to the Love and the Light.

There were other enlightened beings sent here to help spread the word to other cultures about the higher power of the universe. God is so big. God would not limit himself to one culture, or race.

We are all connected to this energy of God. We are not to let religious icons stop the flow of understanding about love and light and Holy Spirits. NOW IS THE TIME.

Everyone needs to learn how to know God within. It is time for you to learn how to know, and use God in YOUR life. God wants to talk to everyone daily so we may have heaven on earth. This is the only way to stop the fear, the violence, the ego madness, the ego-based insanity, and stop the dark (negative) forces we have here on this planet.

"GOD IS WITH YOU WHEREVER YOU GO'- JOSHUA 1:9

"All things can be done for the one who believes."- Mark 9:23

**Brise's story:**

## PARENT'S DYSFUNCTIONAL/UNLOVING, BITTER, HORRIFING DIVORCE-POT, ALCOHOL A FEW OTHER DRUGS, SMOKING, and PARANOIA

Brise came in suffering with a hurting heart, and neck pain. I could feel the physical tension and pain in his body. Drugs were not making him laugh anymore. Drugs and alcohol were not helping ease his pains.

Drugs were keeping him in and around others who were using.

Brise was in fear, loss, and confusion. He was an innocent child, who, nearing adolescence, lost his mom. His dad had taken him away, because he wanted to hurt her. His father had tried to commit his mom. His father spent years threatening his mother's life, and also threatening to hurt Brise and his sister, if his mom did not obey his dad. Brise's father also tried several times to kill his mom, but she got away. The father wanted the children to hate the mom so they would not look closely at his behaviors. He spent years away from them, lying to them about his work, and his bisexual behaviors, and drug addictions.

The wounds and pain were deep. His father used fear, drugs, and money to manipulate his own kids. The father used similar methods to distract, and keep the mother of his children from leaving. Brise found his father using drugs, and all his father's friends used drugs, and they were not so bad, were they? Somewhere in his heart he knew how badly his mother had been treated. He hated his feelings of inadequacy, helplessness, fear, frustration, and rage. He wanted relief from his pains, so he started smoking and drinking, and doping. More choices were poorly made, more problems developed, more horrible feelings needed to be erased. He felt lost with no way out.

**Somehow they all thought they needed to take drugs to be happy**
**Somehow they all seemed to think they needed drugs to get high**

**Somehow they all seemed to think they needed
drugs to get by
Somehow they got lost along their way
Somehow they started to use drugs to measure
their day
Some how the problems were not going away
Somehow the more they would use
Somehow the more they would confuse
Somehow this pit grows deep
Somehow it is time for a faith leap**

"The Lord your God will make you abundantly
prosperous in all your undertakings."-Deuteronomy
30:9

So here Brise was at his wit's end. Drugs were not
the way. He remembered a tiny spark inside. There
must be more. There must be a better way. The
confusion was becoming unbearable. The drugs would
not stop the fears, and the problems were not going
away. He had nothing to lose with trying
Hypnotherapy. After going through all the myths, and
misconceptions about being hypnotized, he felt very
comfortable about the process. He knew he could get
up and walk out anytime. He knew he would only take
in what was in his highest good for him. He knew he
was in control of the entire process.

Brise went into trance quickly. I started to do an
addiction recovery script release program. All of a
sudden he said someone was with him. He told me the
fellow made him very comfortable. He asked his name,
but heard only that he was one of his spirit guides there
to help him. He said he was in street clothes. He said

this Holy Spirit had come to show him more about his soul. Then another much older person showed up. This older person caught his attention immediately. He was older, with a long beard, and he was glowing with light. He was almost transparent looking. He spoke to Brise. He told Brise he was God. He told Brise that he needed self-love. Brise was also to learn how to receive.

He then showed Brise a tool in his hand. This tool had a shape of an open boomerang. Brise remembers this object to be a type of metal. God then proceeded to take this object and throw it straight toward Brise's heart. Brise then left his body. He watched from a distance while this object went into his heart and proceeded to roll him over and over on the ground like a ball. Brise watched as a third person who looked like him, rolled on the ground with this object inside his body. This object was now part of as his heart.

All of a sudden he stopped rolling around like a critter, and came back to the chair he had been in before the object struck him. Instantaneously, Brise went back into his body. He shook a bit, and noticed the pain around his chest was gone. He then relaxed even more. Then he asked God, "What next?"

God shifted over closer to one side of him, and his spirit guide moved to his other side. God and the guide took both of his hands. These wild, yellowish colored, energy rings started to spiral all around him. They were in an energy type of vortex. Then before he knew it, Brise started to fly off with God and his spirit guide. He told me he was in outer space. He could see another planet that had remarkable architectural structures, and glowing light beings. He felt strange, and a bit afraid.

God said, "You are not ready yet," and took him back to my room. He came out of trance so quickly, without any hesitation. This was his first introduction into astral traveling.

Brise was not sure what had happened to him, and was having trouble believing it all. His heart did not hurt anymore. No drug was like this. LSD was a bit. Yet, the weird vibes around LSD can be very unpredictable, and cause many repercussions with off-balanced choices while under the influence. This was the best-altered state he had ever experienced, way better than any drugs, and he had done many types of drugs to get high.

COULD IT BE TRUE, THAT ALL DRUG HIGHS WERE ALREADY IN EVERYBODY'S BODY? Could it be true that you do not need drugs to go to the unlimited and omnipresent world of God? Could it be true that God is unlimited potential, unlimited knowingness? Could it be true God is so cosmic that learning how to use you soul's energy you can get in touch with this power that is beyond this galaxy. Could it be true that this energy of love and light is for us to use to better ourselves, so we may have the kingdom of heaven here on this earth?

Could it be true that God did make us perfect just the way we are? Could it be true that awakening your spiritual knowledge will bring you all the joy, peace, and abundance you deserve as a child of God? Is Meditation a way to tap into this energy? Spiritual hypnotherapy with a gifted technician can certainly help you on your path.

"Did I not tell you that if you believed, you would see the glory of God?"-John 11:40

"My mouth shall speak wisdom; the meditation of my heart shall be understanding."-Psalm 49:3

"Do you not know that you are God's temple and that God's Spirit dwells in you?"-Corinthians 3:16

"The blessing of the Lord makes rich, and he adds no sorrow with it."-Proverbs 10:22

## GOD SPEAKS TO ME! By Herbert J. Hunt

GOD speaks to me! In accents sweet and tender, His promise comes through life to be my guide; In pastures green and pleasant paths to lead me, With rest and shade the quiet stream beside. Thanks be to thee, O everlasting father: For all my wants Thou dost aye provide!

God speaks to me his voice so reassuring, that if I am called to tread the shadowed vale, I'll fear no ill; His rod and staff sufficient to cope with foes, no matter what assail. Thanks be to Thee, O everlasting father. With thee to bless, I must, and shall, prevail!

God speaks to me! O let me gladly listen to words that cheer me all along life's way. His healing balm assuages every sorrow; My cup overflows with mercies new each day!

Thanks be to Thee, O everlasting Father: Within thy house I'll dwell in love always!

# PART THREE

# MEDITATION

MEDITATION, WHAT IS IT? Meditation is spoken about in many religions throughout the world. Most all the major religions speak about the process of learning how to meditate. COULD IT BE TRUE THAT IF WE LEARN HOW TO MEDITATE PROPERLY, THAT WE WILL NOT HAVE TO MEDICATE? We can learn that when we feel the need to medicate, it means it is time to meditate. PRAYER, HOLY BREATH, AND MEDITATION ARE THE WAY TO OPEN UP TO GOD!

Meditation, done properly, can also help you get in touch with your higher power. Meditation can help you listen to God after prayer. You learn to use meditation as a way to help you open your chakras. The more you learn how to use meditation for relaxing, the more you will be opening your heart chakra for divine guidance. Divine guidance will keep you in a soft flow, so you can go about your day more in flow with a true, natural glow. Many people need to have a Spiritual Hypnotherapy session first, before they can meditate on their own. Gifted Spiritual Hypnotherapists are experts who can help you connect to a deeper understanding about meditation. Meditation without a guide is somewhat like a massage that you give to yourself. A self-massage is nothing compared to a good massage with a gifted, trained massage therapist.

Meditation is usually more productive after a master spiritual guide has helped you awaken to your soul. Meditation is easier after you have experienced a connection with your Holy Spirits.

# TRUE CLIENT STORIES

## Tim's Story:

## ANXIETY, DEPRESSION, AND DRUGS

Tim came in suffering from anxiety and depression. More and more situations were making him feel either very depressed, or extremely anxious and somewhat paranoid. He had spent most his life running from his feelings to drugs--mostly pot--for help. He admitted using pot, cocaine, and alcohol. Tim finally went in to see a doctor for help to stop his suicidal bouts of depression. The pills helped a couple of times. Then, about the third time he flipped out. The drugs were not working, so he upped his own dose. This made him feel more insane, so he went to drink away his sorrows. Tim was so out of control he did personal and property damage. (Wish all the newspaper stories would print about the drugs and alcohol used by all the criminals, and all the people who get committed to the psychiatric wards.)

Tim had nothing to lose, and everything to gain. Why not try this? He had been more eager to take some drug, than try Hypnotherapy. He was more afraid of Hypnotherapy than he was of taking a drug, even with all kinds of horrible side effects, both physical, and emotional from drug use.

Drugs are like dynamite waiting to blow, especially with the wrong chemistry of certain people, with their entire unknown, stuffed feelings and total denial. All Hypnotherapy is self-hypnosis. The subconscious will not take in any thing that would harm its own system, because everyone's subconscious is hooked to a higher power, to God. (Thank, God.)

Tim knew he was addicted to pot. He felt he needed his POT daily. Tim also used a few pills/prescriptions, and alcohol to control his unwanted feelings. He went into deep relaxation and trance quickly. His spirit guide Ralph came to help him. Ralph told him he would be able to help him relax, and to let go. Ralph had been with Tim for 6 lives. Ralph could help Tim deal with all three of his addictions.

Ralph explained, that whenever Tim needed help, he could ask for Ralph to help him, and he could listen like he was now through his relaxation and breath work. Ralph could gently give him guidance that would help relieve the confusion around any trying situation or life challenge. After all, Ralph was attached to Tim's soul. He knew more about Tim than any other person, for he was always with Tim. Ralph could also look into the future for Tim. Ralph was one of Tim's Holy Spirits.

Ralph also told Tim not to wait until his depression, anxiety, or, his paranoias became desperate. Ralph told Tim he could help guide him into healthy choices. He told Tim that he must have faith enough to ask for help, hear the answer, and follow the loving guidance. Ralph told Tim he could learn how to talk to God and that he must learn how to believe in himself. Tim must learn why he was feeling his feelings, and let go of them to God, to ask for God's help, and listen for the divine guidance.

Then all of a sudden, Tim says, "Hello there." I asked Tim who was there now? Tim said, "It is Amy. She is here with me. She is my Joy guide. She has been with me for the past 6 lives, also. Amy says I do not need drugs to be happy. Amy says all I have to do to be happy is to learn to call her name for help, and listen to her for her guidance, and she will show me what to do, or where to go, or who to call to help me change my feelings."

Amy could help direct Tim to more happy activities in his life. She knew how to make Tim happy. Amy and Ralph were Holy spirits there for Tim. They would help him follow God's will, not his own limited old habitual free will. Both Amy and Ralph would be there to help Tim understand his Dream symbols. Amy and Ralph would sometimes be the very guides responsible for a certain nightmare. The law of the universe is that Holy Spirits cannot override the free will, except when asleep. They knew why each symbol was given to Tim during his sleep.

Nightmares are very important! The guides try to help you when you have a nightmare. They are not trying to scare you; they are trying to help you notice something important. All Nightmares are given to each individual to help them see something they need to pay attention to.

We are all children of God. We forgot. We lost our trust, and faith in God's guidance. It is time to remember to use God more everyday, every step of our way. With out following God, it is so very easy to follow temptations. "Here take this. This will make you feel better. Pot is an herb. It is good for you. Pot is so much better than alcohol. You should try it. Pot will help you open to God. Pot will make you feel better when you feel sick. Pot is a good medicine." On, and, on… "Have sex with me tonight. I love you. Oh just forgive, and forget all the abuse from me, it wasn't so bad. You needed it. You deserve to be treated like scum. You were bad to me. Take revenge for another brother or sister, or lost child, you will feel better. You are stupid. You follow me. Do as I say or I will hurt you, or kill you."

Many of these comments come out of druggies, even just potheads. All potheads have used other chemicals, and are stuffing feelings and abusing themselves, or others. Potheads are not naturally balanced people, so their choices are also going to be off balance. They are admitting that they are not happy the way they are. They are admitting they need some drug to get high, to be happy. They do not like the way they are feeling. Pot does not heal, drugs do not heal, and they mask deep-rooted problems that must be faced with truth. Only with truth, and by understanding your feelings, can these problems be healed.

Many have been through so much fear, and hurt from trying to trust others that they are lost, and confused. When people are feeling lost, sad, and confused, they are vulnerable, and easily tempted. They are easily led astray, because they are looking outside for their answers. God wants you to have what you put your intention on. When you allow your intention to go towards a lot of negative thoughts, you help enable people of negative energy (darkness) into your space.

*Learn about people in your life, who their true friends are. Do you get a sick feeling around them? What do you feel about a new mate's friends?*

There are so many people that are lost in negative energy habits. Fear will beget more fear. There are dark people that children must be aware of. Children must learn that if they feel odd (bad) about someone there is a reason they feel this way. Children must learn to find a safe feeling person to talk with about their feelings at a very young age. All feelings are about different "vibes" that each of us gives off to one another.

This sixth sense is like when dogs smell each other. We must learn how to pick up and digest these energy vibrations and when we are not feeling "right," we must ask god to help us. We must not let children be swayed by others. They must learn how to stay true to their inner knowingness and feel from their hearts. God's inner direction will keep them on the right path for them--not to slip into someone else's path for them. Children must honor themselves the way they are, to find who they are and their own strength from within, so they can follow their own way and not give their power away.

These dark people use the negative energies to feed themselves. You will feel very drained after an encounter with one. Your mind and body will feel depressed, hurt or generally upset. They only get satisfaction from taking others' powers away. Dark force people may try to take your soul. They must be known, labeled for who they are, and stopped. Do not allow this type of energy into your space. Use your knowingness, and put up boundaries. These people are the only real sick ones! They live to prey on the meek, weak minded. They use financial and verbal coaxing techniques to suck you into their "great world." Their way is the way to fame, or fortune, or whatever. They spend their time and money to manipulate you to do what they want, with their ideas, their way.

ON, and on the power struggles go until you bring God in. God is your way to salvation, and truth. God is inside. God is freedom and power. God--not a person--knows how to get you whatever you need. A person has no right to say these things to you.

"Trust in the Lord with all your heart...In all your ways acknowledge him, and he will make straight your paths."-Proverbs 3:5-6

"The truth will set you free." -John 8:32

Scriptures do not say, drugs, or herbs, or some person will set you free.

"But the wisdom from above is first pure, peaceable, gentle, willing to yield, full of mercy and good fruits."-James 3:17

"Take delight in the Lord and he will give you the desires of your heart."-Psalm 37:4

"I will strengthen you, I will help you."-Isaiah 41:1

"The lord, your God, will make you abundantly prosperous in all your undertakings."-Deuteronomy 30:9

"Do not fear for I am with you." -Isaiah 43:5

"Call to me, and I will answer you, and tell you great and hidden things that you have not known."-Jeremiah 33:3

## Jack's Story:

## EATING DISORDER

Jack's mom called for him. Jack, only 13-years-old, had been struggling with weight problems. I had him write down all his feelings when he was overeating for a week before he came. I also had him write down all his dreams he had been having lately.

Jack was serious about wanting to change, and he was curious about Hypnotherapy.All symbols given to you while sleeping are important to try to remember. The more you ask for help remembering a dream before you go to sleep, the more likely you will remember it. It is best to keep a small light, and a pen near your bed, and jot down part of it during the night. Maybe use a pen light. Dream journals can be very helpful. While sleeping, the conscious brain is asleep, or the ego is asleep, so God's guides can try to help you. These guides cannot over-ride free will. Yet, when you sleep, free will is asleep.

Jack knew that food was not fulfilling him anymore. He knew he was overeating due to an oral pacification type syndrome. He was getting fatter, stretching his stomach, trying to get happiness out of his food. He was trying to satiate all his stressful feelings by overeating. The extra weight was starting to bring him down physically and emotionally. The extra pounds made him feel lethargic, and this led to more depression. This made him want to eat more to stop feeling depressed.

A lot of children in our culture received food to distract their emotions. Some infants were not given enough sucking time. They were not given enough time with a nipple, or a pacifier. Oral pacification conditioning responses show up later in food addictions, and smoking addictions. When some people get upset, they remember from childhood getting something put into their mouth. Extra pounds can also feel like extra protection.

Jack started our conversations with his dreams. Jack's first dream had his best dog friend, Andy, in it. Andy had died. He had a special bond with Andy. Andy had died from sickness in old age. When Andy came to him in his dream, he was healthy again. His eyes were clear, and happy. Andy was lying on a blue and green carpet. His dog was still there to help him not get walked on. His dog was there to help him in his spiritual growth and development.

When a dog shows up in a dream it can also symbolize your friendships. A dog symbol can help you consider your various friends. Are you being loyal, or are you being taken for granted? Dogs are also symbols of concern for protection, and safety issues. Are you feeling safe? Do you need more protection? Are you being loyal to your life mission? Andy's eyes were also very significant to how Jack was seeing the world around him? How was Jack seeing his truth? Was there something Jack did not want to see?

Jack exclaimed, "Now I see more clearly why my dog came. I now understand why I had the feelings I was having when I would overeat." Jack went on to list his different feelings he knew he had when he would overeat. His truths came out. He was having feelings of not being safe. He was worried about his dad's safety. He felt his mom was gone too much, and this added to his feelings of not being safe. His friends had been making fun of him. His friends were not being loyal at all. His girlfriend had also left him. He was arguing with his brother and father.

Jack had one other dream to explore before going into trance. His next dream had symbols of flood, ice, animals, cows, a truck, a trailer, a ditch, driveway, and sick and dying people. Jack came to understand that his emotions were becoming overwhelming.The ice signified blocked emotions that were beginning to surface. He was drifting without inner direction. He looked closer at the animals, and saw these cows. The cows were trying to show him his tendency to go along with the herd, that his true nature was to want to be placid, obedient, and not question authoritative figures. He knew he must question his father, and brother, even though he did not want to.

The truck and trailer that were getting stuck in the ditch symbolized his overeating, and being stuck in the pattern of overeating. Jack was in a rut, (a ditch) with his over weight problem. He knew he could not get his truck and trailer out by himself. He knew he could not move these loads by himself.

Jack was overweight because he allowed himself to over eat when he did not want his feelings to surface. He would try to freeze his feelings (ice). He would block his feelings, because he knew they were not with the herd. His feelings would surface, and he would freeze them, or block them with food. He saw sick and dying people. This was to let him know he would get sick if he kept all these burdens stuffed. He would stay in the ditch (the rut he was in). Jack had to see that some of his relationships must die, because they were so unhealthy (sick). Death in dreams usually means transformation. Death in a dream often symbolizes old patterns and programming dying, to make space for new growth.

Jack was now ready to go into trance. I started with a slow induction process. The breath is the most important human element. The breath is the phone line hook up to the higher powers. The more you open the breath lines, the more you open up the chakras, the more you open up the chi energy lines for receiving information from the universe. The more you let go of free will, the conscious brain, the more the angels can guide you. The more you can relax and let go to God, the more God can help you. God is part of your inner advisor.

I then proceeded to take Jack into his own sacred space. Jack found himself in a room with a couch. The room was shaped like a dome. There were windows high in the dome roof. Jack said he could see lots of stars out side this large window. He said his dog Andy was with him, just like in his dream. Andy was young, and healthy again. Andy was there to help him feel safe, relaxed, and to let him know he was not suffering anymore. Andy's eyes were clear again, as in his dream.

Jack then mentioned his dad was now with him also. I asked him to talk over all his feelings with his dad. Jack started to talk to his dad about his fears, and his frustrations he was having with him being gone so much; especially, with his mom also gone. He started to feel afraid, so I asked if he believed in Jesus. He said yes. Before he finished the yes, Jesus was in this room with them. Jack was then able to talk to Jesus, in front of his dad, about all his concerns.

Jesus helped Jack talk with his dad. Jesus told Jack to call upon him anytime, anywhere whenever he needed help. Jesus told Jack he was always there to help him, he only needed to ask. "After you call on me for help, you must learn how to listen for my answer, and have faith in my guidance for you." Jack then thanked Jesus for all his help, and his dog Andy for coming. Jack took a bit of time for the subconscious to integrate all the information he had been given into the conscious brain.

Hypnotherapy works like this: When the information is given in trance, and incorporated with the waking state, behaviors change. Whenever Jack starts to feel like overeating, he now has another inner guide saying, "Come talk to me about your emotions. Do not stuff your emotions."

Jack has free will, or he can now call on Jesus. Jesus will tell him what to do or say, to help him. Jack must learn to have faith in what Jesus tells him to do. Choices, faith, trust, are now the only true ways for Jack to let go of his emotions and get proper guidance. Jesus can help Jack have such a fulfilling life! Jack will not need to overeat. Jack will not feel he needs to stuff or satisfy his emotions. Jesus can help Jack choose better friends and activities. All these new choices bring better mind, body, and soul balance into harmony. Harmony brings feelings of peace, love, and joy. Jesus can help Jack do more fulfilling things with his time.

"Look at what is before your eyes."-2 Corinthians

"It is your father's good pleasure to give you the kingdom."-Luke 12:32

"May the God of hope fill you with all the joy and peace of believing."-Romans 15:13

"We walk by faith not by sight."-2 Corinthians 5:7

"I am with you always."-Mathews 28:20

"As a mother comforts her child, so I will comfort you."-Isaiah 66:13

"You …are in me and I am with you."-John 17:21

"I have said these things to you so that my joy may be in you, and that your joy may be complete."-John 15:11

"To set the mind on the spirit is life and peace."-Romans 8:6

"Then you shall see and be radiant."-Isaiah 60:5

"If you have faith the size of a mustard seed, you will say to this mountain, 'Move from here to there,' and it will move, and nothing will be impossible for you." -Mathew 17:20

"Know that I am with you."-Genesis 28:15

"Remember, I am with you always."-Matthew 28:20

### J.S.'s Story:

## CHILDHOOD ABUSE

J.S. found me through a friend. The universe had brought several wounded women to Betty. Betty knew I would be able to teach these lost souls how to get their own power by teaching these women how to let go of their hurting bonds from past wounds. I would help them learn how to see, feel, hear, and know their angels. I could help them learn how to let their own divine guides save their lives. Their own divine guides would help show and tell them how to heal and be happy and become whole.

I can help teach them how good their lives will become. I also (thank-you, God) get to explain how this knowledge will help change people's lives. When you learn how to remember to stay focused on your gifts, and your unique soul purpose, the universe will rush to meet you more than half way. The universe will help you balance, and get you into your power flow that is right for you. New choices will open.

J.S. was remembering a weird childhood. She also wanted to know why she kept finding herself in sexually abusive relationships. J.S. wanted to learn how to make better choices. Her father had put his hands onto her private parts many times. Our private parts are considered off limits throughout the world.

Our trust, and boundaries in life choices are connected to these personal property issues. When a child is sexually abused, there are many problems later in life.

These problems come as a side effect from this sick adult behavior. The sexual abuse of children must stop. People all must learn to <u>love themselves, so they can love others--not be perverse with them.</u> Only when people are truly open to God's wonderful, loving guidance, will they make choices that are good and healthy for them.

The side effects of childhood sexual abuse are far reaching. All of these adults experience trust issues. They tend to over trust, or have no trust. All their boundaries in relationships are off balance. All have some degree of unhealthy self-esteem issues. Some revert to masochism or sadism. These behaviors can be around sexual acts or just by the individual to him/or her self. These are deep wounds that need to be dealt with.

These long standing wounds that have been festering inside a person for years, take a few deep, somnambulistic trance sessions. These trance sessions can be the way out of old patterns of behaviors.

The old analytical psychotherapy can keep the person thinking about their wounds for years. We are learning that whatever the human brain thinks about can make it grow. Our thoughts help create our reality. There is an old saying about, "Be careful what you ask for." All activities start with a thought.

When people only react to stimuli with the conscious brain, they've limited their choices to what they've been subjected to while being nurtured as a child. This ego brain is so very limited. During the waking state, the computer brain functions are limited by what it has seen, heard, smelled, touched or tasted. Dysfunctional behaviors children have experienced are stored in their bodies or their brains.

All these unloving, negative situations affect the human body or mind. The more people experience violence, abuse (sexual, or physical), and other negative patterns of unloving behavior, the more wounds they will carry. All physical, and emotional problems come from this lack of love. Most people do not love themselves. Most people suffering so many emotional wounds are kept talking and talking, and reliving these wounds. The more they talk about the wounds the more they stay with the person. What we put our attention on grows. Drugs will not heal these wounds. Most often people have tried to escape the thoughts about these hurts through drugs. Our society has taught people that if you do not feel well then take a drug, or have a drink. All choices while under the influence of drugs or alcohol are off balance; so, more wounds start to develop.

HYPNOTHERAPY CAN HELP YOU HEAL emotionally and physically.

Scientists have known for years we are only using 10% of our brain. We have another section that is the subconscious part. This part of the brain is attached to our sleeping state. This part is attached to God. This part is attached to our soul. Our souls are eternal.

We must start to use this part of our brain more to help us heal, and to grow more spiritually (joy, peace, love) within. The history of how we cope with our feelings, and unloving behaviors on this planet must change. There is still too much anger, rage, revenge, lust, violence, and other abusive negative activities and vibrations happening.

The news should make it mandatory to trace all criminal's drug and alcohol use. The news should make it mandatory to track the drug and alcohol use of all the people admitted to psychiatric wards. Drugs, and alcohol use will not heal emotional or physical wounds.

So back to my client, J.S., and how she overcame her childhood abuse problems. She had been attracting men who were like her father. She wanted to please her dad even though she knew it was wrong. As long as she kept these deep feelings about herself, and her childhood alive, she kept pulling these types of men into her life.

She would not feel good about the situations they put her into sexually, so she would take pot, and sometimes drink. By numbing her feelings, she would escape her pain temporarily. She kept looking for acceptance and love from people who did not love themselves. You cannot give what you do not have.

J.S. knew the importance of keeping a dream journal. She knew that many of her dreams had significances for her to pay attention to. She was aware that her spirit guides and angels were giving her messages while she slept.

The first dream she brought up was the one where she was naked by a fence. She was on a small one-way road. There were several men on the other side of the fence, looking at her, trying to get to her. She realized that she needed to put up better boundaries between herself and other men. She knew she also needed to stop being so vulnerable to them. The road she was on was confining her to one way of relating to men (sexually). She could see she had no real boundaries, and she felt limited in her life direction (the narrow, one way road).

J.S. had a second dream she wanted to look into, before she went into trance. The symbols she remembered seeing in this dream had to do with a newborn, a rattlesnake, a dandelion, and a heart. The release of her newborn had to do with her gift to the world. Her own rebirth was starting. A new phase in her life was coming. A new beginning was starting for her. The rattlesnake was to symbolize temptations. J.S. needed to remember that some temptations could be deadly for her. The dandelion was a false flower. The dandelion was to signify all the weeds in her mind. She had to get rid of all the weeds in her mind, so she could flower. The weeds were all the negative, unloving, unwanted, hurtful memories she no longer wanted to be so attached to. The heart was to help her remember to follow her heart for true love.

J.S. was ready to learn how to let go to God, so God could send her soul guides to help her. She went into trance quickly. Her sacred space was full of green light, and green foliage. She also saw lots of flowers, and berries. J.S. said she saw a beautiful soft, loving woman. This woman was called Matilda. Matilda was an angel who had been with J.S. for 4 life times. Matilda was there to help her heal. Matilda wanted J.S. to see a rainbow, a spider, and the sun. She told her to look for green people, and she was to work with a live craft. She also showed her dragonflies and fireflies.

J.S. found the sun to symbolize the God within, the eye of truth. The sun brings forth life; it nurtures and sustains life. The spider was to remind her about the webs some people weave to trap her. She must learn to create her own life web. When you do not make your own web, you may easily fall into someone else's web. You need to be the architect and the builder of your own life.

You have your own unique reason for being here. When you create your own life story, from within, you will find a rainbow. The rainbow is to help you find the end of your difficulties, and despair. The symbols of the dragonflies and fireflies were to help J.S. to understand kundalini power, life force.

J.S. needed to purify all her negative thinking. She needed to confront all her fears, so that she would open herself to her higher knowledge. Matilda told her to look for the green people. Colors are very important. Colors are attached to a type of energy. The four major archangels, have very specific colors. All people have auras. (The colors of the rainbow are the colors emanated by our chakras, in divine order from the bottom to the top). The Energy of God is so perfect! The reason J.S. was to look for green people was because she needed to heal. Green is the color for healing and new growth, hope, balance, peace, and serenity.

J.S. was in so much need, and so open to God's help, that 4 other spirit guides came to help her. Ali Ishmael came to her. He told her to use the light, and tend her garden. She was to use her God's light within. This would be her power, her way to have her own garden. Her garden needed tending, and nurturing, and weeding. Her garden was to symbolize her fruits from her labors resulting from her work growing and learning. He would be there anytime to help guide her in this manor.

Next came Jacob. Jacob told her he was her warrior. He could help her set up healthy boundaries for herself. He would be there to ward off her father and other intrusive men. (She must remember to ask, spirit guides cannot over ride free will).

Next came Ezekiel, to help J.S. with a spirit resurrection. He told her he could help her to resurrect a new spirit. She could truly have a fresh new start.

The last spirit guide that came to her was Ramah. Ramah reminded her to be of light. Ramah pointed out to her people of stone, and then showed her playing with monkeys. She found this to mean that she needed to be more grounded. She needed to find people who were more grounded. She should stop mimicking others, whose behaviors are not grounded. Stop the monkey see…monkey do. Ramah had been with J.S. for many lives, and he would help her find more grounded people if she would ask him for his guidance (Ask, and ye shall receive, otherwise spirit guides can not over ride free will.)

J.S. can now learn to love herself. These holy spirits are with her 24 hours a day. They know (because they are connected to God) how to exactly help her. They are omniscient, and omnipresent with her. They can help guide her into all she needs to have a loving, abundant, healthy, happy life. You are never alone; have faith and trust God's divine guidance for you.

Now the challenge was for J.S. to believe what all she had been given. She needed to learn how to trust these guides, in various situations, and to ask for their assistance. This is so different from how we were raised. We were raised to keep busy, make goals, work, work, and only pray when all else failed. We have been taught to do as we were told; we were not taught to honor our feelings. Most of us were hurt deeply by someone who said they loved us, and then turned around and abused us. We came to understand hurt came with love. We came to understand that no one seemed to understand or care about us. Some of those people who took our power, and hurt us, would confuse us more with the love word. We all need love, that is all that matters. You have heard and hopefully know, that money cannot buy you happiness! Money cannot buy you love! Money cannot buy you health!

Healthy people have self-love, and other loving relationships in their lives. We must have love to have health, and happiness.

"God is Love."-1 John 4:8

"Create in me a clean heart, O God, and put a new and right spirit in me."-Psalm 51:10

"God is the keeper of the key that unlocks the door to my blessings, I step forward to accept that key and to open the door. Surely goodness and mercy shall follow me all the days of my life."-Psalm 23:6

"Let me hear what God the Lord will speak, for he will speak peace to his people, to his faithful, to those who turn to him in their hearts."-Psalm 85:8

"To set the mind on Spirit is life and peace." – Romans 8:6

"So God created humankind in his image."-Genesis 1:27

"Do not remember the former things, or the things of old."-Isaiah 43:18

"Call to me and I will answer you."-Jeremiah 33:3

"The light is with you."-John 12:35

"This is a message you have heard from the beginning, that we should love one another."-1 John 3:11

"God...Richly provides us with everything."-Timothy 6:17

**Judy's story:**

## CHRONIC MEDICAL PROBLEMS

Judy's ailments were: several broken bones, various sprains (chronic strains), low back pain, neck pain, shoulder pain, headaches, sinus problems, allergies, abdominal cramps, M.S., numbness, tingling, and chronic depression.

She was also on several drugs for the depression, more drugs for sleep problems, more drugs for hormone replacement, and even more drugs for pain.

I must say here how very, very, very, very important it is for anyone on any drugs to go to a pharmacist and find out all the possible side effects from each medication they are taking. Also, make sure about all the side effects that are possible with any known combination of the drugs you may be on. All drugs have side effects. Everyone's body chemistry and food intake is different. How can anyone know exactly how your system with your genes will digest food, much less drugs?

Everyone must realize that drugs are for crisis intervention only. All the American Medical Association work is for crisis intervention, not maintenance, or prevention therapy. On-going drug therapy is deadly if you consider the side effects. These side effects can happen, and they do happen.

There are so many alternative medical clinics now happening. These clinics can help you stay young, and healthy for a long, happy life. These clinics are there to help you before you are in a crisis. They can prevent you from going into a medical crisis. MIND, BODY, AND SOUL WORK IS TRUE HEALING WORK. Most people do not even know that we have a soul. Most people are unaware of the mind-body connection, much less a soul connection. When you talk of soul work, most people do not have a clue. We are learning about how the mind affects the body. We are also learning how the body can affect the mind. Learning how to do soul work can help balance both the mind, and the body.

Judy wanted to learn how to use her higher power to help her with depression, and with her physical problems. First she gave me a bit of history, as to how she got to where she was. Her father was an alcoholic. Her mom was an enabler. She tried to become hard-hearted, to protect herself, but she would be overcome with fear. She felt mentally dead. She had suffered from abuse, and felt sinful and dirty. Her dad committed suicide and left her with a numbness that was complete in all aspects of her life. This numbness was destroying her body and depressing her mind.

She had tried conventional therapy to no avail. She was willing to try a new process with no known side effects. (Hypnotherapy has no known side effects—what do you have to lose?) All you might lose is old baggage, old patterns, old hurtful beliefs, old worn out habits, and fears. YOU STAND TO GAIN YOUR LIFE, as you were meant to be: happy, and healthy, and sharing your divine gifts, and your soul purpose.

Judy knew she had nothing to lose, and could walk out any time she wanted. She was just going to try this process for curiosity, mostly. Any help would be appreciated at this point. She knew she must let go of her past. All the emotions, thoughts, and feelings surrounding her abuse had to stop. She wanted to be happy and healthy. She wanted to have all her relationships be more honest, so she could feel safe and loved.

When Judy went into trance, her guardian angel came and told her not to fear. Her guardian angel told her she was protected, and that she was never alone. Her guardian angel was there for her whenever she felt scared. Her guardian angel had so much love, and compassion for her. Judy had never felt this kind of warmth, love and compassion before from her parents or her friends. I felt a shift in the room, so, I asked, "What was happening?" Judy said she could see another person off in the distance. She felt comfort and love from this other being also. She asked this being to come closer. His name was Samuel. Samuel could help her relieve all her depression. All Judy had to do was ask for him. Samuel would tell her what to eat, where to go, and activities to take part in to relieve her depression. Samuel had been with her soul for 8 lives. He was so glad she was ready to listen to his perfect, divine guidance for her. She was never alone. Samuel was always there to help her, anytime, anywhere. Samuel said by listening to his guidance she could clear up all her emotional and physical problems. Their knowledge, and wisdom to help Judy was unlimited. All she had to do was ask from her heart for help, and then go into breath (-to relax) and listen for their divine direction. Learn how to PRAY, GO INTO BREATH, AND MEDITATE…LISTEN.

"I will restore health to you, and your wounds I will heal."-Jeremiah 30:17

"Know that I am with you and will keep you wherever you go."-Genesis 28:15

"I want their hearts to be united in love, so that they may have…understanding and…the knowledge of God's mystery."-Colossians 2:2

"In God I trust, I am not afraid."-Psalm 56:4

"It is that very Spirit bearing witness with our Spirit that we are children of God."-Romans 8:16

"Keep on doing the things that you have learned and received and heard and seen in me, and the God of peace will be with you."-Philippians 4:9

"Remember, I am with you always."-Matthew 28:20

"To keep understanding is to prosper."- Proverbs 19:8

### Bee's Story:

## A curious teenager, COULD YOU MEDITATE TO GET HIGH?

My next client came out of curiosity. She knew nothing about God. She knew nothing about meditation. She was just curious about hypnotherapy. She had several friends who were suffering from the insanity of drug and alcohol abuse. Was there another way to get high? Everyone wants to get high. How can people be free when they think they need to have drugs, or pot, or alcohol to relax or enjoy themselves socially?

Bee went into trance. A bright glowing light appeared. She felt frightened by the power and unusual nature of this light. The light was Golden Yellow. It was Archangel Uriel. Archangel Uriel is bright yellow. She comes when someone needs help with his or her life goals, and dreams. She comes to help people be relieved of past burdens, and during times of disasters. She comes to help when someone needs to feel calm, and more peaceful. Whenever they (any of the Holy Spirits) feel that they are scaring you, they dissolve.

They are the opposite vibration to fear. They are from love, and light energy. The Holy Spirits come to help you, not put more fear into your life.

Bee saw some trees, a few birds, two people she knew, two more colors arrived: blue, and yellow. Also, she was shown some clay, and a beetle.

When Bee came out of trance, she realized how much she enjoyed the space she was in. She had never felt so relaxed before, not ever. She was also very intrigued as to this altered state she had gone into. This altered sate was fun, and relaxing. What was it?

Bee then discovered that the colors were Archangels. Both Archangels Uriel, and Archangel Michael had come to help her. Archangel Michael's energy takes on a bluish color. He can cut old ties to negative energy patterns (habits). He can help cleanse your heart by cutting old ties to fear. Archangel Michael was there to help her remove all her negative fears. The oak leaves were telling her to remember her strength, her endurance, steadfastness, her power, wisdom, solidarity, and majesty. The number 2 was to remind her that she had a subconscious mind that could help her with her receptivity. She could either double her weaknesses or her strengths. The flock of birds she saw around her was there to remind her not to be a gossip. Also, she was to watch out for catching the blame for others.

The clay was another sign to help her. She was to remember that she had the ability to shape and mold her own life. The beetle came as a sign about her spiritual awakening. Bee would be able to get in touch with her eternal knowledge. Through this knowledge she would be able to shape her own life. All she needed to do was let the angels help her. This relaxation high, and 'TRIP' she went on was better than any drug trip by far!

"So deeply do we care for you that we are determined to share with you, not only the gospel of God but also our own selves."-Thessalonians 2:8

"I have said these things to you so that my joy may be in you, and that your joy may be complete."-John 15:11

"If you do not stand firm in Faith, you shall not stand at all."-Isaiah 7:9

"Lead me in your truth, and teach me."-Psalm 25:5

"We look not at what can be seen but at what cannot be seen; for what can be seen is temporary, but what cannot be seen is eternal."-2 Corinthians 4:18

Take note here of these words from a hymnal song by Saxby, Herbert J. Hunt and Timothy R. Matthews, titled, "Infinite Wisdom Guides My Way":
Infinite wisdom guides my way; My path appears bright as day! God leads me on, and gives me strength, assured I shall arrive at length. 'Tis love divine that prospers me, Health and all good abundantly; With substance rich my life is blest, And in Gods's care I find sweet rest. In conscious union, Lord, with thee, Thy blessing now is given to me; The heavenly windows open wide, My utmost needs are all supplied!

**Manny's Story:**

## MAJOR LIFE TRANSITION

My next client was going through a major life transition. A divorce after 20 years of marriage is a major life change. You need all the help you can get to make the right choices for everyone involved. She was so afraid of a punitive God. She felt so scared that God wanted to punish her for not being a better wife. When all the while, she was trying so hard to be a good and loving wife. They had grown apart through the years. She came to find answers to help her feel her feelings, and get to a place of change in their dead relationship.

She started to feel she was dying in her marriage. Manny was not sure she wanted out, she was used to these numbing feelings toward her mate. The spark had not only gone out, it was becoming a physical and emotional drain to stay with him. They both needed to change to make their partnership work. You cannot change someone else, you can only change yourself.

Manny knew she needed to make changes. It had come to the point that she would make them with or without him. This is where changes start. Manny was afraid to go to God, because she believed what the Catholics had taught her about marrying someone till death do you part. Now what to do? To die, or to leave and live? She became very confused as to her true feelings. Parts of her remembered the good times, and how he had been a good father to their only child. He was not all bad, that was for sure. What happened to them? Maybe some counseling, and time apart would make their relationship change?

Love can do anything. While Manny was struggling with this mid-life crisis she tried conventional psychotherapy to no avail. They also made her feel sick by suggesting she needed to go on drugs. Her feelings were not from a disease, they were real. She needed them validated and understood. She felt more and more confused by all the differing beliefs, and counseling she kept receiving.

Everyone's life story is so unique unto their karma, and other life lessons. Everyone's gifts, and soul purpose, is also very unique unto there own soul. Only God, the Holy spirits–angels--really know what is best for you. The problem is that we are so far from God! We feel so separated from His divine guidance. When we need help, we should have been taught to ask for God's help.

Manny decided to try to go inside and just see what might happen to her with a Hypnotherapy session. She was ready to let go and let God guide her. Manny went into trance quickly, and found herself in a blustering snowstorm. She felt she was going to die from hypothermia, when she saw a faint light guiding her towards a rock bluff. She followed this shimmer to find a cave. Inside this cave was an old Sage. He was one of her spirit guides. She felt so safe, and comfortable in his presence. His warmth of person was nearly as great as the actual fire's warmth. She asked him for help.

He did not speak to her in words; yet, he made it very clear to her that she must learn how valuable her feelings are for her true survival. Manny learned from this old sage that she must learn how to pay more attention to all her feelings. Her divine guidance would come through to her through her feelings. All her answers, from God, would come in a clairsentience form. Manny knew she must learn how to receive God's guidance this way.

When she came out of trance she realized her life was in a snowstorm. Her emotions were blocked, and frozen. The way out of the storm was to learn how to understand God. She also knew that this old Sage was there with her to help her feel her truths. This Sage had been with her many lives. He could help her follow the right feelings that would keep her on the healthy safe, good track for her.

Manny could now learn how to follow God's will or she could follow her old ego's free will patterns. This old sage was a holy spirit. He was part of her soul. Would she learn to trust him and her heart feelings? Or should she go about in fear of her own deep feelings? Should she doubt this whole experience? Fear and doubt were not helping her love herself. Was this experience shown to her like a dream, really true?

She had been taught the spiritual answers were in words from a book, or must come from a counselor, or priest, not from inside herself. She was not special enough to talk to God herself. Manny believed God would only talk to priests. She thought God only talked to special people. Most all people feel so far from God. They think that if they learn the words a preacher teaches from a book written by men 80 years after a prophet's death they can learn how to be spiritual in their daily lives. This is how far we are from our own connection with our daily soul's connection to the love and light energy of this planet.

All our souls are connected to God. God is a part of our subconscious brain, the part scientists know we are not using. This part of the brain is open for divine guidance while we sleep. This is why dreams are so important. The ego, or free will, is asleep so the spirit guides can come to help. Drugs and alcohol make this state very numb. This is another reason not to use drugs or alcohol. It is time to wake up to use our own divine, God-given spiritual guidance within. Stop looking outside for all the answers for your soul purpose. God is inside of you. God has the wisdom you long to feel and follow.

"Lead me in truth, and teach me, for you are the God of my salvation.' -Psalm 25:5

"Remember, I am with you always."-Matthew 28:20

"For everything there is a season."-Ecclesiastes 3:1

"Then an angel of the Lord stood before them, and the glory of the Lord shone around them."-Luke 2:9

# ABOUT ONENESS AND EVERLASTING LOVE

## About Oneness:

Another hymnal song by Carmen Mosier, titled, "Oneness":

I now let go, there's nothing to fear
I now let go, there's nothing to fear, I now let go, there's nothing to fear.
I now let go there's nothing to fear.
I realize there is only one power. I realize there is only one power.
I realize, I realize there is only one power.
I realize I'm one with one.
I realize I'm one with one.
I realize, I realize, I'm one with one.

How, why, when, and where did we get so far from love and the light of God? What happened that took us so far away from daily happiness and truth? Why can't people learn to share and care for each other? There is enough abundance if we could all learn to share. We are not here to be so separated. Why do we wait until it might be too late to ask for help? What happened to the words: honesty, faith, and trust? Why do people fear God? Why do we wait so long before we cry out for help? God will help us find joy, if we would just ask. Why don't we ask God for direction for joy, instead of only for rescue?

After we get so desperate that we cry out for help, we forget to listen for the answer because we do not have faith that God is there. We are so separated from God. Everyone must learn how to talk to God, and listen for God's guidance everyday. Only through God will you find your true way, path.

Most all religions teach children to read a book to find God. If you cannot read, or understand parts of the scripture you are dumb, or must go to a priest who will tell you how to understand their interpretation of a certain scripture. Most religions keep people separated from God through another prophet, or book. Most religions teach that you need a priest to learn how to understand God. To learn about God you must know how to read a writing that was done by a group of people, usually all men. So God has been mostly written about and by, and for men, especially the Bible. The Bible has some great passages, as do all the Holy Scriptures written throughout the world by and for various cultures.

What if you cannot read? What if you know your priest to be an evil person? What if your religion has taught you to fear God? Why do you think there are so many different CHRISTIANS? Why do you think people have to have so many different ideas about Jesus? LOOK AT IRELAND-Catholics fighting PROTESTANTS.

All over the world there are SO MANY WARS OVER RELIGIOUS BOOKS. ALL THE RELIGIONS OF THIS PLANET MUST LEARN TO TEACH LOVE. NOT WORDS FROM BOOKS, WRITTEN BY PEOPLE, just people (mostly men). God is not a written opinion on a book page. Any one prophet cannot contain God. God cannot be contained by a specific religion or culture.

Jesus answered them, "Have faith in God."-Mark 11:22

"God created ALL HUMANKIND in his image."-Genesis 1:27

"The light is with you."-John 12:35

JESUS DID NOT WANT PEOPLE TO GO AROUND FIGHTING ABOUT GOD. Jesus only wanted to help teach people that God was inside of each of us. We are all brothers and sisters. Love one another. If people do not love themselves, how can they love someone else? Jesus wanted people to DO UNTO OTHERS AS YOU WOULD HAVE THEM DO UNTO YOU.

Everyone lives to have love. No one I have ever met wants his or her children to go to war. Let's get together, and stop war! Some think they must take love, or buy it, or it comes in a pill or a drink. Because of all the religious separation from God, we think we can only find God outside of ourselves, from a certain book, or a certain lover, or a certain drug, or a certain activity. God is part of your soul. God is connected to your breath. Remember your spirit! Remember your reason for coming here. Everyone has a purpose, and a reason to be here that is good. Everyone is connected to this unlimited LOVE AND LIGHT ENERGY OF THE UNIVERSE. God is so beyond any book, anywhere. GOD IS OMNIPRESENT. GOD IS OMNISCIENT.

## Everlasting Love:

Another old Hymnal song, "Everlasting Love," by Clara H. Scott and Helen L. Manning:

Ever lasting Love enfolds me, omnipresent, change-less, true;
Satisfieth all my longings, Makes both to will and do.
I am here the father's witness, mighty words of truth to speak;
Banish error, sin, and sickness, Lift the burdens of the weak.
Everlasting love enfolds me, Omnipresent, changeless, true.
Shadows flee before faith's brightness, Hope springs up with buoyant tread;
Health and strength are my companions, No more weakness, pain, or dread.
Power comes to me in the silence, fills my soul with rapture,
Faith proclaims o'er earths dominion wisdom shines with jewels fair.
Everlasting love enfolds me, omnipresent, changeless true.

## TRUE CLIENT STORIES

## Manny's 2<sup>nd</sup> Hypnotherapy session:

## DIVINE GUIDANCE FOR MAJOR LIFE TRANSTIONS

Manny's second Hypnosis session was also very enlightening. She went to a familiar yard where she saw someone hanging out laundry. Then she saw a bright light. Looking closer into this light she saw a chieftain, wearing a headdress of feathers. This chieftain was the one from the cave. He was there before, to keep her from dying during the snowstorm. He was a shaman.

There was a small log house nearby. He took Manny inside. After stepping inside the door, this tiny cabin turned into a mansion. Each room he took her to had a different glow and color to the lighting. He then took her to a room with a fireplace, and gave her neck massage (she had been suffering from a sore neck). She started to drift off, and she visualized a place where there were other holy spirits, dancing and happy.

She asked about her soul purpose, and was shown a view of a huge window on top of a mountain. When she looked through it, she saw down to a valley below. She had such a wonderful feeling in her mind and body. She asked why this shaman had come. He told her without words that he had come to show her how much she had inside of her that she was not using. He told her that he would continue to guide her to the right place so she would not have a pain in her neck.

He told her that she could always remember how it felt to have him guide her to each room, and this is how by these feelings he would guide her directions. She would need to ask for help and feel his answers. Manny could feel for his presence when she was in doubt. Her shaman would be there only if she were on the right path.

All signs and symbols given in trance are there to show people something important about their life. All dreams and past lives and holy spirits can teach you more about why you are alive. Manny realized that the laundry was shown to her to help her clean up inner aspects of herself--mostly her self-esteem issues. He showed her that what may seem small on the outside was huge when looked at within, with a spirit guide's help.

By herself, her resources were very limited. With the spirit guide's help her resources became massive. She had a place to go to actually get rid of the physical pain in her neck, and become so relaxed she could be open to her spiritual guidance. She also saw the Holy trinity. She found this to be a sign that she could find herself, mentally, physically, and spiritually in this trance state. She could get clear seeing from her higher consciousness (the mountain top) to all the valleys (low places, and moods she had) from all the different rooms (aspects of her higher consciousness). She had a place to go to rise above all her self-esteem issues, challenges, and fears. She saw a clearer picture of her life.

Manny is learning how to go inside herself to feel for her divine guidance from God. God is there during every challenge we go through, trying to help. We just do not have faith, or know how to ask, and then listen to this unlimited wisdom for us.

"The kingdom of God is among you." –Luke 17:21

"All things can be done for the one who believes."-Mark 9:23

"For we walk by faith, not by sight."-Corinthians 5:7

"You show me the path of life. In your presence there is fullness of joy."- Psalm 16:11

"Even though I walk in through the darkest valley, I fear no evil; for you are with me; your rod and staff- they comfort me."-Psalm 23:4

**Cindy's Story:**

## ANXIETY AND DEPRESSION

Cindy came in suffering from years of anxiety attacks and depression. She was also struggling with alcoholism. Cindy knew she needed help to make changes in her life habits.

First, she needed to understand why she reacted to certain situations the way she did. She had two children of toddler age. She felt depressed by their behaviors and interests. She did not see the similarity of how her own mother had raised her. She was repeating many of her mother's ways of raising children. Her mother was also very limited in her creative parenting skills. Her mother only knew how to keep a baby safe, warm and fed.

Cindy was getting very bored with the baby stage of development, so she did as her mother did, which was to eat, eat, and eat. Her life, and her kid's activities were all about food: shopping for food, preparing food, and eating food. Her mother was stuffing food for all ills--have a treat and go eat. Her father, whom she adored, would have a drink whenever he felt he'd had a bad day. Cindy realized that her father had taken on drinking to cope with his depression in life.

Cindy's mother was using food to pacify her feelings (stuffing them) and her father was trying to drink his away. None wanted to feel their feelings. Cindy's father became so addicted to using alcohol to escape all feelings, that he became unable to handle even casual social affairs without drinking. He died of cirrhosis of the liver at a young age.

Cindy felt so sad, lost, and confused by his dying. Her mother drifted further and further from her own reality that she started to live her life through her daughter's experiences. Cindy did not care for her mother's intervention in her activities. Cindy's mother was not there to support her. She wanted to control Cindy and Cindy was starting to hate her mom. She realized her mom was an enabler. She also felt her mom could have saved her dad.

Cindy's mom also controlled her with food as a child. She would tell her how fat she was, and must not have a treat. Then when she needed help, and someone to talk with, her mom would get her a treat instead. Cindy felt her body was bad; her self-esteem was dropping and she ate more and more when her mom would say not to. She drifted further from her mom. She left school. She ended up getting married quite young. She was in a relationship with a man who was unavailable (a lot like her dad). They both started to drink socially. She found herself drinking more like her dad. She also found that she was using food to pacify her kids' time. She knew she was becoming what she had been taught; yet, she knew this is not who she wanted to be. The habitual patterns were in place. She was doing what she was taught to do as a child.

CINDY'S ANXIETY WAS DEEP. She knew she was becoming what she feared the most—like her parents! Cindy's depressions came from this knowledge of impending doom. She was doomed if she was to act--or react--in life like her mother or father. For her to be like either of her parents meant only one thing: Doom. To not live would be better than living an empty life. She felt so lost. Everywhere she looked, homes were filled with drugs and alcohol instead of talking and doing family activities. All the social gatherings had liquor and pot or other drugs.

All the relationships she found around her were keeping hidden feelings, and secrets away from each other. So many people were being untruthful about their feelings. Childhood secrets, and wounds were everywhere. Most were trying to forget their past, and not able to be happy in the now. There was a common energy of "Lack" around her.

The energy of Lack, secrets, and darkness from childhood traumas, and horrible dramas must not escape, so the habits continue, and the horror stories, and negative energy increases, and so do the drugs to numb the feelings, and lack of talking, and lack, of truths, and lack of self-love perpetuates more distance, and more confusions that lead to more misunderstandings, that lead to the drugs, and alcohol, to stop the pain from us all.

Everywhere she looked parents were using and abusing someone or something, to get high, to get past what was not from love. Everyone was looking to a pill, to a drink, or a food, or simply going to pot. Truly haven't you heard, how great pot is? The Rastafarians kill their lungs to get high to get by. To get dopey is to get high (to get numb to get by). This is why there are so many "bys." Dope is here, here to stay, as one of the drugs of choice today. It makes you lethargic and easy prey for those who want your choices to be their way. Sexual perverts, and child molestation is on the rise, due to all the (oh, WHATEVER–when an innocent child gets too "loaded").

Drugs, alcohol, and cigarettes, and food along with money can corrupt even you. These are Satan's tools for his prey. These temptations can bait you and lead you so far away--away from the love deep inside of your heart. You become a point on Satan's dart, looking harder outside yourself, hoping you'll find your way to success. The more the drugs, pot, or alcohol you take the deeper the pit, and the harder you will fall. The longer you are down the less chance you'll survive this precious gift of life that just passed you by. ***By.***

Cindy knew now why she would get so anxious, so worried, and so full of fear. The more she would recognize similarities, the worse she would feel, and the more she would use food (her mom's coping mechanism) or alcohol (her dad's coping mechanism).

She was brought up Catholic with the idea that God was to be feared. Her mother told her she was sinful, so she felt she could not go to God because he would punish her.

She went for conventional therapy, only to be told she should take drugs when she became too anxious. The drugs would calm her down. She was also given a prescription for sleeping disorder, and a different drug for depression. The side effects became apparent enough to cause her enough inner doubt that she drank more (sometimes with the drugs). She became more dependent on various drugs, and alcohol until she nearly went to the hospital for good. Enough, enough, enough!

RELIGIOUS BLOCKS are so harmful. Religious blocks can cause more damage than drugs. Why go to God if your own parents won't listen to you? Why go to God with your problems if you think He might punish you, especially for those who have been abused?

She had no positive role models to look to for help. She needed more ideas on how to have a better time as a mom. Our society has taken the MOST, THE MOST, THE MOST important job on this Earth plane, and humiliated it. Stay home mothers have been shamed into taking on a career outside the home. This is insane in itself. How dare people of this time have children and not want to be with them? You only have a few years of your life while they are small. It is over before you know it.

Our society must remember mothers and teachers, and all humanitarian service people more. The world will only come to peace when all people remember to feel their feelings, and ask God to help them (not use drugs or alcohol, dope or food) to numb their feelings. We will only have heaven on earth when everyone learns about their spirits, and how to come to God's will.

Happy people do not hurt others. Our SOCIETY MUST HONOR GOOD MOTHERS, TEACHERS, AND OTHER HUMANITARIAN SERVICES' PEOPLE, so kids will want to become like these role models. Take monies from all the defense departments of the world, gambling casinos, lottery, drugs, alcohol, churches, firearms, and the Donald Trumps and Bill Gates of the world, and redistribute, and share the monies, and power to have better, more loving role models. Drop these monies into the more loving disciplines and schoolings. THE LOVE ENERGY OF THE EARTH PLANE FOR COMPASSION AND SHARING MUST CHANGE!

# HOW TO BREAK THE OLD PATTERNS

First you must see the problem. You must feel, see, and truly understand the cause and effect of certain choices. Cindy knew she wanted to make changes in her life. She was so controlled so much of her life, she was sure the only way to cope--to live--was by what others were doing, or what others told her to do.

So few people understand the concept that God made people like Him. God wants everyone to feel fulfilled. God also wants people to take their own power back. God is a part of everyone. All people can learn how to let go to God and find all their perfect answers. Everyone can learn how to connect to God, to listen for His perfect advice for every need a person might have. God knows exactly how to help you with every life challenge, suffering, or frustration, or anger...absolutely no feelings or situations are too big for God to help you.

What is even better is God knows what is best when you need any advice, even about what turn to take, what food to eat, what would make you happier,

God is omniscient, and part of your breath. God is with you everywhere for everything--all you have to do is ask, breathe on and into it, then LISTEN, LISTEN, LISTEN from your open heart. This is faith. God is here for you, for everyone.

Now, the question would be if Cindy would be able to go to God. She feared God from her childhood. Finally, Cindy went into trance, to a sacred safe place. She saw a door, and felt beckoned to go through it. The other side was pure white light, this soft wonderful light of God. Her whole body softened, her breathing was deep and comfortable. Tears gently flowed from her eyes as a soft smile came upon her face.

The light told her to go with her flow more, to let her life flow more from her heart desires. She was told to follow her heart to new activities that were available to her, and her daughters. These activities would be more fun for her and her daughters. These newer activities would be around dance, and music, and art in such a manner that she would be much happier, and interested in the activities, as were the mothers there.

She also was told to find information from the library about more books. Reading would be another avenue for she, and her daughters, and new friends.

Cindy knew in her heart that one of her major problems was not enough mothers doing any interesting activities with their toddlers. Most were just putting up with them, and doing careers while their toddlers were in day care.

An angel materialized to help her know that she was never alone. Cindy's angel was there for her always. Her angel went on to tell her not to worry about her body image. Her body image would change when her other more fulfilling activities started to change. Cindy's angel said she would help her stay tuned to her feelings coming from love. She would help her learn how to follow love, so she would have more love in her life. The cause and effect, Newton's third law of Physics, would come into play for her if she would give her self more love. She would do more loving activities, and thus more love would be around her.

Drugs and alcohol are too far from the natural flow of cause and effect. Drugs and alcohol are so unnatural for true highs that they can keep you in some serious problems for your whole life. Cindy's angel reassured her that she could truly help her find a more fulfilling life. She must ask, from her heart, and listen.

Cindy said, "Here comes another fellow in a robe. His name is St. Frances." He said he had been with her soul for many years, he was so glad she had come home for help. He told her about many of the dreams she had in her life. He knew all about each one-- perfectly. He told her that several other Holy Spirits were there for her, also. He explained that Holy Spirits come to you in dreams because your free will is asleep. Otherwise, they can only come to your aid when you ask. Holy Spirits cannot override free will.

This was such an experience for Cindy. Her angel came out of trance with her to knowingly go with her to help her on her life journey. God's Holy Spirits know best, perfectly--perfect for each of us.

We have chosen long ago (the apple with Adam and Eve) not to listen to God. Our free will is running amuck on this planet. What must it take to get people back to themselves? What will it take before people reach out to God instead of trying to take something by force from someone else? God will give you what you need. No one should want to hurt anyone, anymore. You do not have to hurt others anymore. You can avoid so much hurt, by learning how to listen to God's direction for you every step of your way.

"See what love the father has given us that we should be called children of God, and that is what we are."-John 3:1

"Above all, clothe yourselves in love, which binds everything together in perfect harmony."-Colossians 3:14

"When Joseph awoke from sleep, he did as the angel of the Lord commanded him."-Mathew 1:24

"Our inner nature is being renewed day by day."-2 Corinthians 4:16

"Well then, does God supply you with the Spirit and work miracles among you by doing the work, of the law, or by you believing what you heard from God?"-Galatians 3:5

"To the thirsty I will give water as a gift from the spring of life."-Revelations 2:16

# TRUE CLIENT STORIES

## Casey's Story:

## CHILDHOOD ABUSE, AND STUCK BEHAVIORS

My next client came after a Unitarian Universalist gathering for solstice. We were doing a native American (Cherokee) Ritual. This ritual was done to help people be tied together in thankfulness. Each person would keep hold of a piece of the golden thread as the end with a red orb tied to it kept getting passed from person to person. The thread made a glistening spider web as each person said a thankful prayer. After holding and stating your specific prayer of thankfulness you look around the circle and throw the red orb to whomever you are drawn to throw the red orb to. The spider web kept getting more and more intricate as the stories went on and on.

In Ted Andrews book, *ANIMAL-SPEAK: the Spiritual & Magical Powers of Creatures Great &Small*, he has a wonderful section about spiders. This book is one of the best that has come to me to help me understand how all of God's animals in the northwest talk to you. Whenever an animal or spider or any of God's living creatures come into your world, they have come to tell you something about yourself. They have come into your space to help you look and listen to your divine connection through the mother earth plane. All insects, birds, and animals have a reason for being alive, and in your space. Whenever I encounter an insect, reptile, or bird, or animal of this northwestern

American area I immediately go to look at Ted Andrews book to help me understand why a certain creature has come into my space. If I have a vivid dream about a bird, reptile, animal, or insect I will meditate on it, and check Ted Andrews Animal-Speak book. I also check my dream books, and see if I get an "ahha syndrome" (feeling).

I know more and more the truth and beauty of the mother earth connection and the Father (cosmic-love, and light energy) connection everyday I look and see with clear eyes. There are so many signs around you. Everything is trying to help you. Mother earth is talking to you and so is God. It is so worth it, to wake up and see, and feel the perfection of you, just the way God made you. EVERYONE HAS THEIR OWN BEAUTY, AND GIFTS, AND REASON FOR BEING HERE JUST THE WAY GOD MADE YOU. YOU DO NOT NEED ALL THOSE OTHER THINGS OUTSIDE, TO MAKE YOU FIT HERE, ON THIS EARTH.

God made you a certain way, with specific gifts, and a soul purpose that you are here for. You must learn how to see, and feel, and know, and hear all the beautiful signs around you everyday. The signs are there all around you, trying to help you. Learning how to open to mother earth, and to the heavenly Father (love and light energy) is they only way to come into your truth and balance on this earth.

You must seek to find yourself, and where you fit. FEELINGS, FEELINGS, FEELINGS, ARE SO IMPORTANT!

Feelings are our individual way of understanding the vibrations we see, hear, smell, touch, and taste, and that six sense must be honored in all of us. We must study all about "VIBES."

Casey continued and 12-year-old:

Going back now to my latest client, when we got side tracked about the spider web story. After this group gathering, Casey came up to me and asked if she could come to my office and do a bit of breath work and energy work. She seemed to truly need a bit of time. I said ok. She came out the door with her friend's12-year-old daughter. I was shocked. I told her I did not think it would be appropriate for the girl to come along.

We called the girl's mom and she said it would be okay for her daughter, Lucy, to come along and just sit quietly. She could do some drawing.

I was able to get Casey calmed down and into her breath work, and before I knew it, both Casey and Lucy were in deep trance. Both gals needed help. Seek and ye shall find, knock and the doors will open. Heaven's doors opened wide and quickly for both gals. They were both talking so much about their sacred places, and spaces, and Holy Spirits it was so amazing to me. I was having a difficult time keeping up with both of their situations.

Lucy: (was looking for more guidance, and life purpose than either Casey or I understood)

Lucy was so excited to see her dead grandma, and another young boy who had died. They both had come to tell Lucy not to worry about them. They were just fine where they were. Her grandma told Lucy about her guardian Angel Andrew who would be there for her anytime. Andrew waited in the distance for a bit then came over to Lucy. Lucy asked Andrew about a scary dream she had and Andrew explained it to her.

Andrew asked if Lucy wanted to go see her horse, which had passed away. Lucy loves animals. She wants to be a vet. She said she would love to see her horse, Sky, again. Andrew held onto Lucy's hand and off they went. Lucy was so excited to be whirling out into space inside this light bubble.

When she and Andrew arrived at this planet, Lucy was so very excited. Lucy said, "I have always wondered if there was a heaven for animals." She told Andrew that she was so happy he brought her here. Lucy wanted to become a vet. She said the animals were not all from our planet, that there were other planets they were from.

There were other creatures she had never seen before. They were not from Earth. Lucy told me that the animals were coming up to her and telling her how to recognize certain diseases, and nutritional problems before they die from them. These animals were, in effect, telling her how to be the best vet ever. While she was getting all this information, her dead dog and her dead horse from years ago, came running up to her. They were well now. All the animals and creatures were healthy, but they could show a picture, and explain how to understand certain problems she would see as a vet, and know instantly what was wrong with the animal. (God is all knowing.) Sky showed her also that her real horse at home, on earth was in trouble. He showed her she must watch out for a cougar that was after him. She must put him in the barn at night.

This was a lot for me to believe, all this--OK, now what?

While Lucy was having all this experience, Casey was in a meadow saying my name and to stop being with Lucy, and help her in her sacred space. Casey's Holy Spirit guide had come, but she was so listening to Lucy she lost him. He left, and she was frantic to reconnect with him. He told her his name was Michael. He was an Archangel, and he wanted her to get unstuck, and not be so afraid. She also saw her daughter dancing with a huge crowd of glowing beings. She had let her daughter go spend time with her dad, and she was so worried about her.

Casey reconnected to her body, and all this horrible black color started oozing out of her guts. The entire area below her belly button was oozing out this black color. It was the fearful and dark blocks she had held inside herself for years, because of being molested. She also said she had had many physical complaints in that area lately.

She started to say how much better the area was feeling after purging this dark block out of her. I did not want her to openly let go of too much more than this color in front of Lucy. I asked Lucy how she was doing, and she said she was having a great time riding her old horse around; (she had not heard a word of Casey's story). They were both is such deep trance, and on their own journeys for what they needed for each of their lives to heal and grow.

It was getting late, so I decided to bring them both back to the room for reorientation time before we went our separate ways for the evening. Lucy went into a dark tunnel, into the light, and then came back to the room.

So much happened that Casey asked to come in again, by herself for another appointment. That time she was more able to open up about all the sexual abuse, and alcoholism, and pot use she had been brought up with.

Casey had been labeled manic-depressive and bi-polar. I am so sick of these labels placed on people that are so hurtful, and wrong. With her childhood history, and all the drugs and alcohol to get by, it is no wonder she had episodes of bi-polar states. We made arrangements for another session.

LONG TERM DRUG THERAPIES and recreational ALCOHOL MUST STOP.

This is the millennium. It is time to change, to wake up to your spirituality. There are other modalities out there to help people to stay at ease, and have a good life, and be in flow. The New Age healing arts are a valuable way to actually heal yourself. Music and Sound therapy, dance and other body movement therapies, Art as therapy, Massage therapies, Energy work, Acupuncture, body work, dieting and exercise, and relaxation, meditations, Hypnotherapies, Gardening, new sports, spiritual gatherings, Pet therapy.

There are so many fun and relaxing new ways to enjoy your life. Try new Community Education classes. Is it not time now to use the other parts of our brain? Again the cosmic energy, and knowingness of God is much bigger than the Internet. It is free, and perfectly--perfect just for you. Mediation can help you learn which other Healing arts you may need in your life.

So what if a person gets depressed? One thing is proven about Alcohol. Alcohol is a depressant. People prone to depression should not use alcohol. Try the Healing arts. So what if a person gets manic? Why don't the doctors tell their patients to run a marathon when they are feeling manic? Hell, how far would they go manic? If this didn't stop the manic phase, how about trying some form of rigorous exercise? I bet the manic would be calm before the end of a healthy workout.

Same for all the ADD crap! Those kids just need to learn how to do a sport, or a marathon. Train them, use this energy—do not drug it. God gave these kids a lot of energy; it is special. They are not sick!

PARENTS NEED to go to the pharmacist and get a PHYSICIAN'S DESK REFERENCE. READ all the medications and their side effects before medicating children, or anyone. How can anyone be sure if a medication actually works with your cellular metabolism, and your cellular nutritional uniqueness? Who eats the exact same foods as another person every 24 hours? How can anyone without knowing exactly what is in your blood stream as far as nutrients go, prescribe a drug, and say it will only have such and such for side effects? What all will you eat, drink, and breathe in the next 24 hours? Who has exactly the same DNA? What are the known side effects of what you are taking? Is this medication for your body size, diet, and exercise truly good for your system?

Why not try Hypnosis? There are no side effects. Your higher power will only take in what is in its best and highest good.

All the mental hospitals and jails are not helping these people get out of their disease. Old Habits and patterns must change. They need to find out where they belong, not that they do not, cannot, and will not ever belong! What kind of judgment have certain parts of our society dictated?

How possibly could this type of labeling ever help a person become whole? Again all psychiatric disorders are actually normal reactions for what happened to these people. What happened to these people was actually crazy. These people are temporarily sick from what happened to them. They are not crazy! How some people *cope* with traumas is what seems crazy. Look again: what happened was the cause; they are the effect—same as with all the jail inmates, who have been pushed, hurt, lost, and use violence (like they know, and have seen –experienced, and been taught) to cope with their lives.

Both of these groups have something in common. They are lost. They do not know where they fit. They do not like where others have told them they fit. They do not know how to change their past and make a new way for themselves. Where do they belong? Most religions teach fear of God. They also teach the people if they do not understand the Bible, then they cannot be worthy (or smart enough) to know God. Neither type (quiet and fearful, or angry and violent) was ever taught how to love themselves without any drugs or alcohol. What have we done to our society?

These people need God's help. God is inside. People should not fear God--maybe fear the lack of God, but not God. People do not have to go to church. They do not have to go through a special understanding of Jesus or anyone else. They do not have to learn to read and understand the Bible to have a knowing of God. All they really need to know is: How to PRAY for themselves, let go to God by deep breathing, and LISTEN to God's perfect, loving advice. God will not give you hurtful or fearful advice. God gives only healthy, loving advice. Listen to God from your heart, not your ego.

## Casey's 2<sup>nd</sup> Hypnotherapy session:

Back with my client who was labeled bi-polar: She was fine, and not doing any drugs, anymore. The drugs and alcohol mix made her bi-polar. Now she wanted to understand her feelings, not drug them out. She went into trance quickly and arrived at the exact same sacred space she had been to before. Archangel Michael came again, in the bluish color. He had come to help cut all her ties surrounding her fears about sexual molestation as a child.

Casey could feel this energy release. Casey could feel this huge burden being lifted off her guts, and from her right shoulder. She saw her three male family members who had violated her disappear when she let Michael cut these fear bonds to them. This was an immediate relief of letting go to God. It was a physical sensation, and a visual one also. It was fascinating, and done so quickly.

Then a yellowish glow came forth. The closer she looked inside the coler she could make out a figure.

This was Uriel. Uriel was there to help remove past burdens from her soul. Uriel was also there to help Casey understand how to calm herself whenever she needed to. Uriel explained that she could call on her anytime whenever she needed to feel more calm and peaceful. Uriel could gently guide her to a person, place, or activity that would help her calm down.

Casey needed to ask for help with major life decisions; this meant she must ask for her master teacher to come and help her. There he was, her master teacher was Jesus. She was then able to ask Jesus some questions about her future choices. These choices seemed to be conflicting within her right now. Before Jesus arrived she felt very alone, confused, powerless, and uncertain of herself.

Jesus was able to clear up all her doubts within a few minutes. She felt without a doubt that his direction was the only way for her. She knew from deep in her heart he loved her. Jesus told her he was always there-- she just needed to learn how to ask, and LISTEN for his divine guidance. Whenever she needed to get some help, her angels and Jesus would be there for her always…anytime, anywhere. They would lead her and her daughter to the right people, and the right choices every step of her way through this life, if she wanted. She must learn to ask, and Listen from her heart, not her ego.

They told her she was loved and they wanted her to be happy and healthy, and have the life she deserved.

### Casey's 3<sup>rd</sup> Hypnotherapy session:

Casey wanted her daughter to learn how to talk to God herself.

The next time Casey came she brought her daughter in with her. Her daughter filled out a medical form that made me want to dowse her charkas, which I did and found a big block over her 3rd Chakra.

The third chakra is located in the solar plexus. It externalizes as the pancreas, governs the action of the stomach, spleen, liver, gall bladder, and parts of the nervous system. The third chakra has to do with personal power. It has to do with the energy around personal emotions, an empowerment. The color from this energy is orange.

Her block around this area was so apparent when dowsing the chakra. Jenny started to open up to her feelings with me. I asked why she was showing such a block about her power. She mentioned that she was feeling very responsible for her parents' divorce. She was frightened by it, and her dad was so far away. She felt very guilty. She told me she loved them both. While in trance she could see it was not her fault. Jenny was able to let go of her guilt. She was able to release herself from her past issues surrounding the divorce. She felt this higher power that would be there to help her. She felt how important she was to this higher source; she was happy, and relaxed.

Jenny came out of trance happy, and hungry--her 7-day stomachache was gone.

Her mom had come in to get help with two major life issues: Casey needed help with divine guidance knowing: 1) should she work on this new relationship she had just made; and 2) what type of life career should she now pursue? (Casey had used the various techniques to find her own answers, she just wanted to go into trance and make sure she heard Jesus right.)

Casey went into trance quickly. Jesus came during her last session. This time she needed to get verification as to the still small voice she was learning was Jesus inside of her. She was still in doubt as to whether or not to listen. She did not trust this newfound voice since her last session. (Most people are so fearful of being taken advantage of–again in their lives, it can be a slow process to learn how to talk to God, yourself, and have faith in his guidance for you. We have been taught for so long all our answers are out there. All the altered states to cope are already inside. All perfect direction for your path is inside.)

She still needed help to get inside, to connect with her soul guides. Casey did not know how to pray and listen for guidance. She felt so betrayed by God for letting her be sexually abused as a child that she had little self-esteem or trust for anyone. When she relaxed and went into deep relaxation and asked for help, Jesus was there immediately.

Her body became soft, and her jaw relaxed, and a soft glow came to her presence. I knew she was safe, and so at "home." Jesus told her not to stay in the new relationship. This man would only be like the others had been, and she would be used again. They talked and talked, most of which she did not care to tell me about. He gave her all that she needed.

Casey came out of trance so happy to know that Jesus was there for her anytime, anyplace—in all ways and always. She must learn how to pray, and listen so she does not get into temptations, and lose her way.

Again, the holy spirits know exactly what you need, but ...YOU must ask for help (they can not override free will), and then you must listen and learn how to hear, feel, see, and know their loving guidance for you. We all have angels, joy guides, and a Master teacher available to us at any time. ASK and ye shall receive. LISTEN and have faith in the loving guidance, so you can learn how to trust your feelings, so you can find your unique way, and so you can have self-love!

# CHAKRAS AND CHI ENERGY LINES AND DOWSING

## CHAKRAS-SEVEN HUMAN ENERGY SYSTEMS, and how they attach to love, and light energy of the universe.

Another aside—a type of a note about the importance of energy: All cells are made of energy. We have an anatomy of our spirit. Dr. Caroline Myss, PhD's book: *ANATOMY OF THE SPIRIT*, explains this more in great detail. Doreen Virtue, PhD also explains, the importance of Chakra work. Chakra work is such important energy work. You cannot heal a person's emotional or physical problems without studying their chakras. Each person's chakra system is a part of his or her soul. To understand the missing link is our soul connection.

Without understanding the soul connection, there will be no healing that is lasting, for a person's body or mind problem. To have health you must be in flow. This energy is part of our soul energy reflected inside each of us. It is an energy that is measurable, (like ultra-sound, and sound waves). This energy is also connected to the chi energy of acupuncture, and acupressure points on the human body. The Chakras can tell you how all your emotional (ego-based) energy systems are working for you. To explain briefly:

CHAKRA = spiritual energy, this energy runs the total length of our spine

Known Facts: This energy has color to it (light energy). The colors are from the base of the spine up: red, orange, yellow, green, blue, purple, and white light. These are the colors of God's rainbow! How perfect!

We are all very affected by sound waves and the Chakras are made up of vibrations of the "C" scale. The bottom chakra is middle C,d,e,f,g,a,b-c, which connects us to the universe.

Art and Music are important to our soul's well being, by soothing our minds and our bodies with colors, and movement. We all need art and or music in our daily lives.

The base of the spine is the root chakra. It governs our physical dimension. This is our energy system for survival, "flight or fight." This area shows how we feel about safety, survival issues, and security. When there are problems surrounding these kinds of issues for a human being, you will find problems with spinal column, kidneys, and adrenal glands.

The second chakra is located in the sexual organs (ovaries in women, testes in men) and is the chakra of creativity. It governs attitudes in relationships, sex, and reproduction.

The third chakra is located in the solar plexus. Self-esteem, emotional sensitivities, and personal power issues are here. The pancreas, stomach, spleen, gall bladder, liver will show signs of problems, if suffering from long-term issues of power, and self-esteem.

The fourth chakra is the heart chakra. It externalizes the thymus gland, and governs the heart, blood, and circulatory system. It helps influence the immune and endocrine systems. This is the center through which we feel love. When we do not have much love for others in our lives, we end up with problems in all these systems. A broken heart is very real.

The fifth chakra is the throat chakra. It governs the thyroid gland, lungs, vocal cords, bronchial apparatus, and metabolism. This is the center for communication, judgment, and expression.

The sixth chakra is located in the center of the forehead. It is better known as the third eye. It externalizes as the pituitary gland. It governs the lower brain, and the nervous system, the ears, the nose and the eye of the personality. This is where we connect to our spiritual nature—or ignore our spiritual nature.

The seventh chakra, the crown chakra is at the top of the head. It externalizes as the pineal gland and governs the upper brain and right eye. This is where we can go and learn to use this center to balance our minds with our bodies through communion with knowing and using god in our daily lives.

Anatomy of the spirit can help you understand your life issues better so you can ask for more specific direction, and guidance from God to keep you in balance, and going in a good flow. This is your best direction for your energy and your spirit. This is how to live God's will, not your old free will, old patterns, old habits, old tapes from your past. LET GO, LET GOD.

## DOWSING:

DOWSING YOUR CHAKRAS! Our bodies are made up of atoms, so they do emit an electromagnetic field. These electromagnetic areas can be measured with a pendulum. You can also learn how to dowse your entire body for yes, no, or a maybe answer from the universe. You use your entire body as a pendulum. The universe will give you very specific movements to indicate to you what is a yes answer, a no, or a maybe answer. You can learn how to ask the universe for help, and you can learn how to feel these answers for yourself. You are never alone, and the universe is always waiting for you to ask for help. Dowsing is a fun way to feel the energy from your higher power to help you make the best choices. The Omniscient power of God is real. The Omnipresent power of God is also real. You can learn how to use this energy for your best and highest good--anytime, anywhere. God wants you to be happy. God knows what is best for you. Dowsing is one way to connect to this Love and Light energy. Prayers are connected to this same energy grid. Sound therapy and light energy are also connected to this energy grid.

You can learn how to dowse your chakras, and your friends' chakras. You use a type of plumb bob or pendulum. You let your friend, or client, or relative get into a very relaxed flat position, usually a supine position. The next step is to hold your pendulum over the different areas of the chakas. Your pendulum will swing one way to signify an opening, and another way to show if there is a block. If the energy is blocked you will feel it. Most people are blocked in very specific areas. They may not be conscious of the deep problem area, because there is another area that they are knowingly stuck. Sometimes the issues at hand overwhelm the deeper problems. The areas where they are blocked may have started in another life.

Another reason to learn how to dowse is so you can slowly build your trust, and faith in your feelings about situations. By learning how to dowse you can learn how to check in with God before major decisions. Dowsing helps you to be more present in your choices, and to feel more of the vibrations that are around you. Dowsing can help you become more aware of your feelings in any situation. Dowsing can help you get the best advice for your long-term advantages. Dowsing can help you double check your ideas about your dreams and your ideas to make sure they came from God, or from Divine Guidance.

# TRUE CLIENT STORIES

## Lana's Story:

## CHRONIC PAIN-PAINFULL LIFE

Lana came wanting pain relief. Her low back and legs were giving her chronic pain. The different pain medications were not working that well anymore. She came originally for a massage. She then realized she needed more than body work.

She realized her chronic pain was a reflection of her life. Her life was becoming more and more painful. She also knew she needed more resources than she had been using. She wanted to try hypnotherapy, to see if it could open more doors for her.

Lana was able to go into trance easily. In trance she found a lot of gray color, like fog. She then let herself go a bit, and a bright blue color came next to her, she got scared from this bright color, so the shimmering color vanished and black came (black, is a sign of fear of the unknown). I was able to help her relax more and let go, and then a pure white, soft glowing light came. The pure white light came in soft tones with feelings of comfort. Lana was able to talk to the light.

This light was the light of God. Lana was able to talk to the light and find answers she needed to know. The light told her she must learn how to listen to this still small voice inside of her, to feel this voice, and follow its direction. This still, small voice would show her the way to happiness and less pain. She was also shown a waterfall, and a bridge to many beautiful colors.

She found the waterfall to symbolize God's unlimited caring, and resources available to her. The mixed emotions from the various mixed colors would all be calm and healed by listening to the still, small voice within.

Lana was told how to listen, and hear this perfect voice for her. Her spiritual discovery started this day. She was to let God be in charge of her life more every day.

"Know that wisdom is such to your soul; if you find it, you will find a future."-Proverbs 24:14

**Larry's story:**

## DEPRESSION AND DRUG DEPENDENCE

Larry came in for his depression. He had been through several drug treatment programs. He just kept sinking into it. He went into trance easily. He was in such need, he was open to any help he could receive. The first angel came as a beam of light. This angel came to tell Larry how to find his true inspiration and follow it. Another holy spirit came and told him to pay more attention to TAO. This spirit guide told him to have courage to follow his inspiration.

The next guide showed up; his name was Octavian. Octavian was his master teacher, and available to him anytime and anywhere. Octavian could help him through any life challenge, and help him make healthy safe choices for himself.

Larry saw an image of himself as a mutant, who was short, squatty, and nagging. This image would go away if he would go across the bridge to the grassy hill, and there would be a whole city available to help him overcome any life challenge. He could then find faith, hope, and trust.

Larry had a most gratifying experience meeting with his soul guides, his Holy spirits. He knew in his heart he could truly trust these spirits to help guide him. This was the voice of his soul.

Larry's spirit was lightened and the depression had been removed by knowing he had a place to go for help. He knew he could pray and listen for this helpful guidance. Just to know that he could let go to a force bigger than himself, and get direction for help lessened his depression.

"Do not worry about anything, but in everything by prayer and supplication with thanksgiving let your requests be made known to God. And the peace of God, which surpasses all understanding will guard your hearts and minds"- Philippians 4:6-7

"For thus said the Lord God… In returning and rest you shall be saved; in quietness and in trust shall be your strength."-Isaiah 30:15

"Keep on doing the things you have learned and received and heard and seen in me, and the God of peace will be with you."-Philippians 4:9

**Betty's story:**

CHRONIC JAW AND NECK PROBLEMS (Post-traumatic stress disorder)

Betty came in with jaw and neck problems. She had years of struggling with anger, frustration, and a desire for revenge. These issues were damaging her emotionally and physically. She was looking at more mouth surgery, and possibly neck surgery.

She decided to have her neck, and jaw muscles released with a combination of massage, and light work energy, and hypnotherapy. She loved it. She then felt comfortable to ask more about deep hypnotherapy possibilities. I went on to explain that it was like a brain massage. Hypnotherapy can alleviate all kinds of pain and discomfort, both emotionally and physically. I let her know that you can let go of deep traumatic stress disorders this way.

Betty found herself in a sacred place. She felt relaxed and open to her soul. Here came Sam. He had her laughing and listening to his direction for her. He told her she must make time for more laughter. He told her to look for work in nature, that she would like the people who worked with nature best. He said the people who worked with nature would be her best friends. Betty felt interested and excited about this information for her.

Then, a woman came up to her. Her name was Samantha. Samantha would teach her how to love herself. Samantha would teach her about her gifts to share. These gifts she already had inside of her. Samantha would also teach her how to give love from her heart, so all her relationships would be happier.

Betty looked very relaxed, yet attentive. She mentioned two more angels were coming. They wanted her to know that she had unlimited loving help from God each day to help her. She only needed to learn how to reach out. They told her they would help her relieve all her POST–TRAUMATIC STRESS DISORDER issues. They would joyfully resolve them for her, and guide her into a new direction. By following her new direction she could let go of all the anger, frustration, and past hurts. She would be free to be more loving toward others.

"Get wisdom, get insight, do not forget, nor turn away."-Proverbs 4:5

"I commune with my heart in the night; I meditate and search my spirit."-Psalm 77:6

"To you, O Lord, I lift up soul; in you I trust, O my God." –Psalm 25:1-2

"Like good stewards of the manifold grace of God, serve one another with whatever gift each of you has received."-1 Peter 4:10

"Be renewed in the spirit of your minds"-Ephesians 4:23

"Thanks be to God for his indescribable gift!"-2 Corinthians 9:15

**Murray's Story:**

**POT AND CIGERETTE ADDICTION**

Murray came in with lung problems. He did not want to mention his pot addiction. Murray was so sure pot was better than alcohol. He wanted to testify that pot was so great (sometimes). He was starting to get heart palpitations, constant lung irritations, and bronchitis, and colds often. He was starting to get apathetic about his work, and all his relationships. His belief that he needed these drugs was taking more and more of his time away.

He realized he was becoming socially dependent on pot, just the same as some people are on beer, and wine or other social drinking. He felt he had to have his pot to cope at any social function. His paranoia was getting worse; also, his apathetic, and lethargic responses to pot were not making him happy anymore. He was considering more drugs, and combining more drugs to get high. He knew his quest for highs was starting to consume most of his waking hours. All his interests, and goals, and activities were falling away in lure of getting and taking drugs.

His short-term memory was nearly gone. His attention span was so spaced out. His hypothalamus was being affected, and sugar cravings were constantly causing diabetic type symptoms. The more he used pot the harder it was to remember conversations. The more his short-term memory lagged, the more social paranoia set in. The more uncomfortable he became with his feelings the more he wanted to change them. He only knew how to use drugs to cope with unwanted feelings. He learned drugs were the only way to escape reality, lighten up, and relax, to have fun.

He felt everyone was using something. He started to notice that when he would get high he would act dopey at times, and others would be able to talk him into doing things he really did not care for. Yet, the pot brought out the attitude of "oh, whatever." This "whatever" syndrome can be devastating on people who do not have boundaries. They become the victims of all kinds of behaviors they normally would question.

ALL ADDICTIONS are an escape from what you are feeling! While you are escaping your feelings, many of your choices will hurt you or others. You are avoiding your healing, and doing damage to yourself or others by using. All users are abusing themselves and others! How did this become "cool"? How did this way of being become fun?

SO HURT, SO LOST, YOUR ACTIVITIES, AND CHOICES ARE NOT IN BALANCE. This is not natural. This is not a natural high. This is not the way God made you to be. This is not why you are here. This is not what God wants for you. This is not the way God meant for you to be full of JOY.

EVERYONE WAS MADE PERFECT and made to have a good time, and a good life here. Everyone has a gift to share, and a reason to be here, now. REMEMBER YOUR SPIRITUAL REASONS TO BE ALIVE NOW! This is the only way to joy, true lasting joy. God will set you free. God loves you, and knows what is best for you. By learning how to feel, see, know, and hear divine guidance you'll truly be inspired and on your path, which is your way for you to find your own love, joy peace, and health, abundance here on earth.

Murray went into trance. He found a guide named Stan who had been with him for two lives. Stan told Murray he could help him stop smoking cigarettes and pot. Stan told Murray it was time to leave them behind. He did not need them anymore.

Murray had other feelings from his childhood that he was not aware of. He found out he had many issues around not being safe. Ruth came. She told him she was his Guardian angel. She would help Murray during times when he felt scared, or threatened. Ruth had been with Murray for four lives.

Murray had other major issues in his life that he needed help with. His master teacher came to him in a crème colored robe. His name was Jim. Jim answered Murray's questions about major life issues for him and his wife. Jim told Murray he was not to worry so much, and to learn how to relax naturally. Jim told Murray he was to take more time each week for art. Jim also explained how he was part of Murray's higher power. He told Murray all the drug highs were already inside of him. Jim went on to explain to Murray that he did not have to spend time or money on drug highs. Whenever he thought about taking a drug, he was to ask for their help first. They would help him get by, and get high naturally, and so much more!

Murray came out of trance so excited, and yet thoroughly relaxed. He was amazed that his master teacher, and guardian angel knew exactly what he needed. Murray knew they spoke a truth that resonated inside his heart (his soul).

"Therefore my heart is glad, and my soul rejoices."-Psalm 16:9

"For everyone who asks receives, and everyone who searches finds, and for everyone who knocks, the door will be opened."-Matthew 7:8

"You will have confidence, because there is hope; you will be protected and take your rest in safety."-Job 11:18

"Remember, I am with you always."-Matthew 28:20

From the hymnal, *Wings of Song*, comes, "I Am Listening," by Sicilian Mariners (A.G. Denning):

I am listening, I am listening For the still, small voice so dear;
I am listening, I am listening, that my heart and soul may hear
All the truth God is revealing to his children far and near.
Day by Day I'm learning something Of the purer, better way;
Day by day I grow in knowledge of the life, the Truth, the way,
How to love and help God's children realize that brighter day.
When the light of truth is shining through my mind and soul so clear;
When my intuition guides me, And I know that God is here,
Then no more can sorrow touch me, then is banished all my fear.
"The spirit of the Lord God is upon me, because the Lord has anointed me; he has sent me to bring good news to the oppressed, to bind up the brokenhearted."- Isaiah 61:1
YOUR FAITH CAN MAKE YOU WELL.

## IN SUMMARY:

Wake up to your soul--REMEMBER WHY YOU CAME! Use energy work, light work, chakra work, dowsing work, DREAMS, PAST LIVES, HOLY SPIRIT GUIDANCE. We can have heaven on earth when we connect to heaven daily in our lives. When your life needs more meaning, or you are chronically ill, or want to have a better understanding about what to do with your time, there are answers for you. You can change, you can heal, and you can be naturally high.

New beliefs bring new attitudes, which bring on change. You have heard "if there is a will there is a way." There are ways to make changes; there are ways to find out about your soul energy, your soul gifts and your soul purpose.

HYPNOTHERAPY, AND MEDITATION CAN HELP YOU FIND YOUR LIFE! You can OPEN TO YOUR SPIRITUAL ENERGY, YOUR SOUL CONNECTIONS, YOUR SOUL PURPOSE AND YOUR UNIQUE GIFTS.

Ninety-five percent of humanity has a heart. Most all people came to the earth plane for good reasons. All people with a heart have a beautiful, fun soul purpose to remember. When you remember, you can then get passion, and love, and balance in your life. Spiritual Hypnotherapy can help you find your soul purpose, and unique gifts you came here to share.

This is the knowledge you need to learn how to follow. When you are following your divine guidance you will be healthier naturally and happier naturally. This is how God wanted you to be, to remember to listen to His will for you, not the ego's will. This is the way to stay in flow with your heart desires that were given to you from the universe BEFORE YOU CAME THIS TIME.

Everyone has a wonderful reason for being alive, and a unique gift to share that will give meaning and prosperity to their lives. People must learn how to FEEL THEIR FEELINGS. FEELINGS ARE YOUR ENERGY GUIDES. LEARN HOW TO HAVE YOUR OWN CONVERSATIONS WITH GOD.

People must learn how to talk about the 'VIBES,' they get from daily living experiences. Double-check your choices, and thoughts. Are your thoughts coming from past fears or inner guidance? Use meditation and dowsing to help keep your information clear and grounded. Ask for help, and breathe deeply…evenly…slowly through your challenges, the breath is the phone line to your Holy Spirits. After you ask, breathe deep, slow steady breaths and listen, listen, listen for your divine guidance. You are never alone. They want you to ask, so they can help you.

You can go back to the part about dowsing in this book. Remember to use dowsing about your choices. Double-check your choices with dowsing. Is you answer from the universe, or from your fearful, ego mind? You can have a friend help you dowse to double check your answers. God is fun energy, good energy for you to use.

People would be healthier if they received good massage work, energy work, sound therapy, or art therapy on a regular basis. Massage and energy work are as important to human health as diet and exercise. People must learn how to use their dreams, knowledge from past lives, and their own connection with the inner voice of their divine guides every day to make healthy choices and find SELF-LOVE.

With all the confusion today, there is only one healthy balanced way out. God is the only one who knows exactly for you. People who are far from their spiritual connection add confusion and negativity to their own lives, and to those around them. The vibrations from lost, dark souls are adding more misery to the earth plane. Negativity, and chaos from the darkness, with the added confusion of drug, alcohol, and eating disorders are adding more and more imbalances around every individual. The energies are so off the natural balance. Too many people are suffering from DIS-EASE every day!

What you think about, and put time and attention on will grow. You are responsible for your thoughts and feelings. Are your thoughts coming through from inner wisdom or from your ego?

Everyone must make new choices, from God's voice first. God's will must come first, not how you were brought up, not from their ego self, not from all the dysfunctional ways of coping with the unwanted feelings.

All feelings are happening to each individual because of Newton's third law of Physics= CAUSE AND EFFECTS. PAST LIVES ARE A PART OF THIS LIFE'S CAUSE AND EFFECT.

Our souls are eternal, so past life information is very helpful. God's energy is attached to you inside your chakras, to your soul, to your spirituality. Everyone must take individual responsibility for their feelings, to understand where their feelings came from, and how these feelings are affecting them in the their daily lives. To balance the mind, and body, you must use your soul connections to God.

Everyone can learn how to feel all vibrations around him or her. Everything is happening to individuals for a reason, unique unto them. Everyone has feelings to help them focus on balance. How can there be balance without knowing your soul connection? Your mind and body cannot become balanced without your soul, without your understanding of your spirituality. You must learn how to use God's energy "VIBES" everyday, and in every way. This is the only way you can have a truthful, happy, fulfilling, healthy loving life!

This is the way to get your mind, and body healed. THIS IS THE WAY OUT OF EVERY EMOTIONAL DISEASE! THIS IS THE WAY OUT OF EVERY HABITUAL ADDICTION! THIS IS THE WAY TO FIND YOUR LOST SELF, TO BECOME HEALTHY AND HAPPY. God wants all his children to be healthy and happy. God made you in his image, perfect. God knows exactly how to help you become healthy and happy, NOW! God made you to be here. God can help your mind, and body flow here on this planet. God wants you to stay centered, balanced, from inside out. This means to ask for God's direction, and listen before you react with your free will mind.

Your free will is limited. It stores hurt, and wounds, and fear, along with many other negative, confusing vibrations (feelings). The truth from God will set you free. This is the way to natural highs, natural balance for each individual. This is the only way to stop the chaos, is to find your self worth in the here and now. Learn how to listen to the guiding wisdom attached to your soul.

LOST, LONELY SOUL'S,
--by Lynn Mystic-Healer

THE BEST DRUG IN LIFE IS LOVE
THE BEST DRINK IN LIFE IS LOVE
THE BEST FOOD IN LIFE IS LOVE
THE BEST SMOKE IN LIFE IS LOVE

WHAT ARE YOU THINKING?
WHAT ARE YOU FEELING?
WHY ARE YOU SMOKING?
WHY ARE YOU TOKIN'?

WHY ARE YOU DRINKIN'?
WHY ARE YOU STUFFING?
WHY ARE YOU DRUGGIN'?
WHAT ARE YOU POPPIN'?

All these habits lead you astray,
Far, far away.
Come out of your darkness-
Come out of your Fear,
Feel your soul's light path
God is always near.
Waiting for you to hear.

DREAMS, PAST LIVES, AND HOLY SPIRITS (ANGELS, MASTER TEACHERS), AWAIT YOU. They are PART OF YOUR BREATH, YOUR eternal SOUL. Find a talented Spiritual Hypnotherapist if you need extra help with your soul connections.

God wants the very best for you. God knows the exact path you should take. God knows your past, and your future. God knows your hidden talents, and your soul's purpose. By learning how to talk to God, you can balance your mind, and body. Make the best choice, by asking God's help first. If everyone would learn how to use God's energy, and omniscient power for their lives, how different this world would be. All answers lie within each person's soul. Happy people are healthier.

Remember to ask (pray), to breathe (deeply and evenly), and then to meditate (listen for divine guidance). TALK WITH GOD EVERY DAY (reach to heaven, not to drugs or alcohol), FOR A BETTER LIFE IN EVERY WAY WITH TRULY DIVINE, NATURAL HIGHS JUST THE WAY YOU WERE MADE TO BE.

# Bibliography

The Holy Bible-New and Old Testament

Silent Unity, Daily Word

Unity Books, WINGS OF SONGS, Hymnal

D. Corydon Hammond, PhD, HANDBOOK OF HYNOTIC SUGGESTIONS AND METAPHORS, An American society of Clinical Hypnosis Book

Doreen Virtue, PhD, DIVINE GUIDANCE, St. Martin's Press

Betty Bethards, THE DREAM BOOK, Element Books Limited

Wilda B. Tanner, THE MYSTICAL MAGICAL MARVELOUS WORLD OF DREAMS, Sparrow Hawk Press

Sonia Choquette, YOUR PSYCHIC PATHWAY, Audio by Nightingale Conant

Ted Andrews, ANIMAL SPEAK the Spiritual & Magical Powers of Creatures Great & Small, Llewellyn Worldwide

Marrianne Williamson, LIVE lectures based on a Course In Miracles, Nightingale Conant

Caroline Myss, PhD, ANATOMY OF THE SPIRIT, The seven Stages of Power and Healing, Harmony Books

Louise L. Hay, YOU CAN HEAL YOUR LIFE, Hay House Inc.

## About The Author

I, Lynn Mystic-Healer, LMT, CHt, have an eclectic background. I grew up in a military family. The military promoted drinking with "happy hour." All military social gatherings had alcohol involved.

I started working when I was ten years old picking fruit. I graduated from High School #13 with high honors, from a class of about 207. I also had one or two jobs all through high school, making all my own spending money.

I married young (nineteen) and in the course of the marriage we had twenty-five homes in two countries. I was an R.N. in rural Oregon and Queen Charlotte Islands in B.C., Canada. I spent over three years living from 12 to 23 miles to the nearest neighbor with winter months of twenty to forty below zero. My two babies, Leah, and Owen, were only nineteen months apart. I had no phone or electricity, and lots of chores: cooking on a wood stove, feeding horses, milking cows, etc. I lived in a sod roof cabin, with a dirt floor, about 100 years old. I went for over two months one winter and never talked to another adult, and my husband would leave me alone–a lot. Somehow, I knew I was not really alone, especially with Leah and Owen.

After quitting nursing in the Queen Charlotte Islands, I decided to stay home with my kids, and help develop an international Wild Gourmet Mushroom Co. The bigger the company got, the more money we made, and the worse our family life became. Our family dissolved more and more year after year. The more I tried to have a family, the more my ex was gone with his boyfriend, daily "pot, drinking, and some cocaine use. Our marriage ended, violently and then we went our separate ways.

I decided to pursue the healing arts again. I was just about to get my R.N. reinstated when the drug book arrived. My heart said no-no-no. My grandfather was a pharmacist, which led my mom to feel there was a pill for everything. My RN work substantiated this whole idea.

Off I went to massage school. I loved the sports injury work training I received, the Repetitive Stress Injury (RSI)-total healing techniques that were being used to heal horrible injuries, and techniques were being developed to alleviate surgeries.

I had a NDE, (near death experience) and realized I must pursue meditation, and Hypnotherapy. The more courses I took about Hypnotherapy the better I felt. Hypnotherapy was the way out of all my old addictive habits, stuck problems, poor choices, wrongful relationships, and soooo much more! It was incredible! I only wanted to pursue the Medical scripting release work when joy guides, saints, dead people, dead animals, Jesus, Buddha, guardian angels, Sages, other angels, and other Holy Spirits arrived to talk to my clients. These Holy Spirits came to help, and they knew perfectly what to say, or do with these various clients to truly help that client be happier, and healthier.

I am now a member of the ABH (American Board of Hypnotherapy) and the OHA (Oregon Hypnotherapy Association). Both the ABH and the OHA are full of various people with M.D.s and Ph.D.s practicing Medical and Spiritual Hypnotherapies. Hypnotherapy works because it puts the ego to sleep, and brings up the Soul power of the person. Medical Hypnotherapy (see my book section for details) now has a medical insurance code #90880.

I love to help people-I thank God I am able to share this information with you, to let you know there is a Cosmic-God energy that is full of omniscient loving light that is omnipotent and omnipresent for you; so you too, can have faith, trust, joy, love and peace from learning how to use your own inner soul power. Your SOUL CAN HELP YOU HEAL YOUR MIND AND BODY PROBLEMS. The SOUL connection is the way to balance the ego and the body for a healthy and happy life.

www.ingramcontent.com/pod-product-compliance
Lightning Source LLC
Chambersburg PA
CBHW022211050726
47590CB00002B/749